Dating for Under a Dollar

301 Ideas

Cover photographs by Keith Campbell

Printed in the United States of America

Dating for Under a Dollar

301 Ideas

compiled by
Blair Tolman

To my best friend and wife,

Tristan

the best evidence I have that
dating for under a dollar really works

For possible future volumes,
send your ideas to

Blair Tolman
1039 East Kiefer Avenue
Fruita, Colorado 81521

Preface

As a teacher who works with teenagers, I am frequently asked for ideas concerning inexpensive dates. In an attempt to satisfy these requests, I have collected hundreds of dates from many creative people that meet these criteria. I am extremely grateful to everyone who contributed their ideas to this book since without them, this book would not be a reality today.

I would like to express thanks to my high school buddies Brett Blake, Chris Tullis, and Mike Florence who taught me that dating doesn't need to be expensive to be fun. Also, thanks to my mother, Marie Wade, and my mother-in-law, Sherrie Thornton, for sustaining me in all of my endeavors and to my wife, Tristan for her constant support, for her editing skills, and for testing out many of these ideas with me. I appreciate the assistance of both Randal Wright and also Brad Wilcox in publishing this work. Finally, I appreciate the encouragement from family and friends as I have attempted to put these ideas into book form.

Contributors

Monte and Gail Atkinson
Brad Bateman
Jaime Bickmore
Randy Bird
Brett and Erin Blake
Darrin Case
Ky Christensen
Dallen Craven
Jarom Dastrup
Erik Dunn
Kyle Dunn
Jason Ferguson
Brian Fleming
Mike and Rachel Florence
Richard R. George and family
John Gifford
Betsy Greco
Erik Groves
Jared Haddock
Daren Hardy
Jena Hardy
Jeff Harmer
Josh Hedrick
Tiffany Holder
Richard Huffaker
Becky Jacobson
Coleman and Barbara Jacobson
A. Todd Jones
Mike and Loretta Klaich
JoJo Kohls
Buck Kolz
Stanley Martineau
Darrin McGowan
Christy Nelson
Brandon Parrish
Justin Parry
Jackie Peterson
Chuck Reid
Jeff Salter
David Talbot
Kip Thygerson
Jayne Tolman
Mark and Becky Tolman
Rick and Perla Tolman
Steve and Lisa Tolman
Tex Tolman and family
Tristan Tolman
Marie Wade
Mark and Chrystal Walker
Adam Watkins
Brad Wilcox
Randal Wright
Brittanie Yeaman
Sasha Yeaman

Contents

What's Wrong With This Picture?

For months, Jason had his eye on Stephanie, his dream girl. Boy, was she a knockout! Stephanie had it all: looks, personality, talent, you name it! He felt ecstatic when she accepted his invitation to go to the hottest concert of the year. This was Jason's big chance; the one date he just couldn't mess up. Boy, would she be surprised that they were sitting on the front row of the special events center. No expense would be spared in his effort to win her heart.

Driving to her house, Jason reviewed his checklist of preparations one last time. The dozen long-stemmed, red roses would surely melt her on impact. His new clothes with the right name tags and professionally styled hair couldn't go unnoticed. Dinner at "Shakespeare's," one of the most prestigious restaurants in town, would definitely express his upper-class nature. A few extra pushups made his sleeves stretch a little bit tighter, and the savory scent of his cologne lingered in the air. Wow! He looked and felt fantastic! Chances were, Stephanie wouldn't even order dinner or look at the performers on stage because her eyes would be feasting upon him.

As he approached Stephanie's driveway, Jason took

one last look in the rearview mirror. He tamed a stray hair and wiped one last bit of shaving cream from behind his ear. Rummaging through the glove compartment, he located the mint breath freshener and shot a quick spray into his mouth. The Lion was finally ready to catch his prey.

So, what's wrong with this picture? "Nothing," you might reply. Everything seems perfect. The roses, the concert, the name brand clothes, the restaurant, everything looks absolutely flawless. So what's wrong? While this date may seem to include every ingredient necessary for Jason to impress Stephanie, what is he trying to impress her with—his personality by planning a fun evening for them to get to know each other better or physical pleasures and spending lots of money on her?

My purpose in writing this book is to suggest that dating creatively and inexpensively offers huge advantages over spending excessive amounts of money on dates. Hopefully, by considering the example of Jason and Stephanie for a few moments, we can learn some tips for planning successful dates in our own lives. Determining the goals of dating will help us in planning impressive, creative, and inexpensive dates.

So, what are these goals of dating? The first is to date frequently. For unmarried people, common sense tells us that dating is a numbers game. The more people you date, the easier it becomes to recognize the qualities you seek in a future spouse. For married couples, dating renews and strengthens romance, as well as offers important time together away from daily pressures. Since financial resources generally factor into how often people date, it makes sense that the less expensive dates are, the more dates people can go on. Obviously, a date like the one Jason has planned could easily cost a hundred dollars. If instead of spending the entire sum on a single date, he saved it and spent only a dollar on each date with Stephanie, he could still afford many more dates with her in the future!

The second goal of dating is get to know your companion better. Dating provides opportunities for people to become more familiar with the interests, feelings, and values of those they choose to go out with. Therefore, dating should be geared to promote communication. In the pamphlet *For the Strength of Youth,* the First Presidency of the Church of Jesus Christ of Latter-day Saints counseled, "Plan positive and constructive activities when you are together. Do things that help you get to know each other. Be careful to go to places where there is a good environment, where you won't be faced with temptation." While Jason's activity did allow for some communication at the dinner table, activities like going to a concert or to a movie don't provide many opportunities for learning about each other, and probably should be avoided for the first few dates. As Jason planned his date with Stephanie, he might have asked himself, "How will this activity help us get to know each other better?"

The third goal for dating is to impress your companion so much on the first date that he or she will hope for and want to accept another date in the future. It is far more effective to impress a date by allowing her to see your terrific personality rather than your thick billfold. Hopefully, the first date with someone will be so much fun that he or she will tell others how much fun it was to date you, even if the two of you never date each other again. When you invite someone on a date, the nature of the activity planned is generally an expression of your character. Creative dates give you a head start in making a statement about yourself. While Jason's date may have seemed impressive to some, how did his personality factor in impressing Stephanie? Hearts are won more often by creativity than by expense.

Since the purpose of successful dating is to find and associate with someone who has a personality compatible to your own, this book is designed to assist in planning and carrying out dates that fulfill this purpose. My hope is that this book will serve as a resource for you as you brainstorm your own creative dates for under a dollar in the future. I believe that the best dates have yet to be created. Hopefully, the ideas presented in this book will help create them. Good luck and good dating!

Chapter One

Activities for Large Group Dates

Animal Farm

The entire group sits in a circle. One person is selected to be the farmer. The farmer is blindfolded. Anyone in the circle who wants to, silently moves to a different spot in the circle. The farmer then kneels in front of one of the people in the circle and names a farm animal. The other person disguises his voice and makes the sound of that animal. The farmer tries to guess who the person is by the animal sound. If he guesses correctly, that person becomes the new farmer.

Animal Mix-up

This activity is a fun mingler. On slips of paper, write down the names of several animals. Use as many kinds of animals as you want groups. For example, if you want five groups of five people each, write five different types of animals on 25 slips of paper, five times each. Put all the slips of paper into a hat and have every member of the group select a slip of paper. He or she will be this animal for the duration of the game.

Blindfold everyone, say "Go", and have them mingle through the crowd of people, attempting to find the rest of the animals in his group. He does this by making the sound of his animal and by listening for other members of his group to make the same sound. When someone finds another member of his group, he must stay with this person and together they continue to make the animal sound to find the rest of their group.

Balloon Blasting

Each participant blows up a balloon to a standard size. Secure each balloon to a rear belt loop. Give each person a rolled up newspaper to use as a blaster. At the starting signal, each person attempts to blast and pop the balloon of another opponent. When your balloon is popped, you are eliminated. Play until only one person is left.

Balloon blasting can also be played in teams. Give each team a different color balloon and begin the blasting. The winning team is the one which pops all of the opponent's balloons first. For even more difficulty, add the rule that players must hold their feet in their left hands.

Body Roll Racing

Divide all players into at least two teams and line them up behind a starting line. Have them lay down with their stomachs to the floor, touching shoulder to shoulder, forming a platform of backs. On the "Go!" signal, the last person on the team rolls up onto the platform and proceeds rolling until he comes to the end. When he reaches the end, he lays down in front of the first person, extending his team's platform beyond the starting line the width of his body.

When the end person rolls onto the platform, a new end person is created. This end person can roll onto the platform as soon as he or she becomes the end person, thus creating a constant wave of bodies rolling across the platform. In this manner, the teams race toward a finish line. The first team to have each team member across the finish line wins.

Blindfolded Fire Brigade

Divide the participants into two teams. Team members sit on the grass one behind the other, all facing the same direction. The last person on each team has a one-gallon milk jug tucked in her lap. Give each participant a paper cup which has ten pin holes poked in the bottom of it. Place a full bucket of water in the lap of the first person on each team. Blindfold all participants.

At the "Go!" signal, the first person in each team dips her cup into the bucket of water and passes it over her head or shoulder to the person behind her. She must dump the water from her cup into the cup of the person behind her. The water is passed from cup to cup in this fashion until it reaches the last person. The last person carefully pours any remaining water into the milk jug. The winning team is the one with the most water in the milk jug at the end of a given time period.

Variation: If you feel like getting dirty, pass mud instead of water. No cups are necessary, just use your cupped hands. Be sure that the mud is really sloshy.

Capture The Flag

This group date is ideally played in a large forested area. Divide the playing area into two equal sections, each about fifty yards square. Also divide the group into two equal teams, and give each team a bandanna to use as a flag. Each team should place its bandanna somewhere in its designated area where it can be best defended from being stolen by the opposing team. Before playing, tie one of each person's hands to one of his or her partner's hands, so that each couple must work together.

The objective of the game is for you to sneak onto the enemy's side, capture its flag, and return it to your own side without being tagged by the enemy. The team which succeeds first in doing this wins. If a couple is tagged, it is taken prisoner and put in jail near the enemy flag. The jailed couple can only be set free by being tagged by a couple from its own team.

Variation: Buy or borrow soft tipped darts and tag the enemies with darts instead of touching them.

Catch-N-Go

Catch-N-Go is a low-contact sport played indoors or outdoors as long as enough room is available. An indoor basketball court is a good sized playing area. Create two teams. Make two goal lines in your playing area, one on each end of the playing field. Play begins with each team standing on its opponent's goal line. A football, volleyball, soccer ball or another type of small ball is needed. Flip a coin to see which team gets the ball first.

To begin play, team A tosses the ball across the goal line. Upon doing so, both teams can leave their lines. Members of team A toss the ball to each other, counting each successful catch as a potential point. The person with the ball is free to run wherever she desires. As in basketball, physical contact between the offense and defense is limited. The ball cannot be swatted away from an individual once she has possession of it.

The object of the game is for team A to throw the ball across its own goal on the opposite end of the field and to have one of its team members catch it. When a team succeeds in doing this, it scores the number of total catches made before crossing the goal. However, if the ball is dropped, batted to the ground, or intercepted during the tossing, team B takes over at that spot. Play to a designated score or until you're too tired to play anymore.

Variation: Instead of allowing the offensive team to run with the ball, allow the person catching the ball to only take three additional steps in any direction.

Circle Squishing

Circle squishing is an exciting activity to see how small of a circle your group can smash into. To play, make a circle on the floor using masking tape. Make sure the first circle will fit the entire group without too much discomfort. After everyone has successfully fit inside the circle with no toes hanging over the tape, make another circle with masking tape inside the first circle and squish everyone into it. Proceed in this manner, seeing how small of a circle your group can fit into. Be as creative as possible: sit on shoulders, make pyramids, or sit on laps to utilize your space as economically as possible. You'll be amazed how small of a circle you can all squish into if you work together.

Variation: Divide into teams and compete to see which team can fit into the smallest circle. For even more competition, time each group as they attempt to squish into a circle. The group with the lowest time wins.

Do You Love Your Neighbor?

The entire group sits in a circle. A person is chosen to be "it," and stands in the middle of the circle. This person approaches any person in the circle and asks, "Do you love your neighbor?" If the person says "yes," the people on either side of her must quickly attempt to trade places. The person who is "it" tries to sit in one of their places while they are switching, leaving a new person to be "it."

If, however, she answers "no," she must say who she does love instead. For example, she might say, "No, I don't love my neighbor, but I do love everyone wearing white socks." At that point, everyone wearing white socks must trade places, leaving an opportunity for whoever is "it" to try to steal someone else's spot.

Elbow Tag

Elbow tag is played in pairs. Link people together in boy and girl pairs at the elbows. All couples should stand in a large circle, with each pair standing approximately an arm's distance from another pair. Select one couple from the circle to start the play. To begin, the girl goes to the middle of the circle, and the boy stands outside the circle. When someone shouts, "Go," the boy rushes into the circle after the girl. She rushes to one of the pairs and links elbows with one of the boys, forming a threesome. The girl on the opposite end of her must release her link with the boy and must attempt to link elbows with another boy while the boy rushing through the circle tries to catch her. If she gets tagged by the boy who is chasing her, roles immediately switch, with her now trying to tag the boy.

Electricity

For this activity, the group sits cross-legged in a circle. Each person holds hands with the people on both sides of them, placing their hands on their knees in plain sight. One person is selected to be "it" and sits in the middle of the circle. Put several slips of paper into a hat, and mark one of the slips of paper with an "X." Pass the hat around the circle, and have each person take one slip of paper.

To begin, the person who drew the "X" squeezes the hand of one of the people next to him. Like electricity, this squeeze is passed from person to person around the circle, each person immediately squeezing the hand of the next person. The person in the middle watches closely, trying to sight a squeeze and find the spark of electricity. When she finds it, the person caught passing the squeeze replaces her in the middle of the circle, and the game begins again.

Fruit Basket

Choose one person to be the caller. The rest of the group sits in a circle on chairs. The caller assigns each member of the group, including himself, a type of fruit. He should use as many different fruits as he wants groups. When the caller calls out the name of a fruit, everyone who has been assigned that fruit must jump up and run to a different vacant chair. The caller attempts to sit in one of the vacant chairs while they are running, leaving someone else without a seat. The person without a chair becomes the new caller. If instead of calling the name of a fruit, the caller yells, "Fruit Basket," everyone in the group must jump up simultaneously and exchange seats.

Furniture Maze

Arrange chairs, sofas, stools, and tables into a maze throughout a room. The more twists and turns you include in the maze, the better. Divide the group into couples. Blindfold the boy and position him at the starting point of the maze. Don't blindfold the girl, but have her standing nearby. Say "Go" and time the couple as the boy attempts to maneuver through the maze. The girl guides him through the maze with her voice by telling him which direction to go. Time each respective couple to see which can maneuver through the maze the fastest. After all the couples have had turns attempting the maze, rearrange it and have the girls go through blindfolded with the boys guiding them.

Giant Twister

This group date will test your level of physical endurance. Make a giant Twister board by painting large circles on a large sheet, each circle about twelve inches in diameter and spaced about sixteen inches apart, in checkerboard fashion.

To play the game, have each person place either a hand or a foot on the colored circle of her choice. Each person then takes turns calling out a new color as well as a movement of a hand or foot. Only hands and feet can touch the board. The last person to fall wins.

Ha-Ha

Ready for a good laugh? I hope so, because if you play this game, you're bound to have one. To set up Ha-Ha, each person lays down, resting the back of his head on the stomach of another person, forming a zigzagged human chain. To play, the person at the end of the chain says, "Ha." The next person must say, "Ha-Ha." The third person must say, "Ha-Ha-Ha." This continues, with each consecutive person saying one more "Ha" than the last person. The goal is to refrain from laughing and to successfully say the correct number of Ha's on your turn. If a person laughs or says the incorrect number of Ha's, he is out of the game and the zigzag chain is made again without him. This continues until only one person remains. He is declared the winner.

Human Cookie Machine

To form a human cookie machine, divide the participants into two equal rows. These rows face each other with each person joining hands with the person across from him, creating a U-shaped conveyer belt with everyone's bodies and arms, along which the cookies will be passed.

Choose one of the ends of the line to be the beginning and the other to be the end. The couple at the beginning of the line becomes the first "cookies." One at a time, they climb onto the cookie machine. The couples forming the cookie machine lift the cookie and toss it forward along the line until it reaches the end. The finished cookies form new links on the cookie machine.

The cookies should cross their arms across their chests and lock their feet together to make their passage easier. Play until everyone has been a cookie.

Variation: Divide the group into two teams and race your cookie machines against each other.

Human Knot

Here's a way to be knotty without getting into any trouble. Everyone in the group forms a circle and links hands. Holding their hands high above their heads, the group walks inward until everyone is standing close together. Then they let go of the hands they are holding and grab different ones. This will form a giant human knot. The group must attempt to unravel the knot into a circle again, without ever letting go of the hands they are holding.

I Love You Honey, But I Just Can't Smile

This poker-faced activity is more for unattached friends than for couples. The group sits in a circle, facing inward. One person in the group sits in the middle of the circle. This lonely for love person approaches the person of his choosing and has three tries to make her smile, each time saying, "If you love me, smile." The person spoken to must solemnly answer, "I love you honey, but I just can't smile." If she doesn't smile after three attempts, he must try his tactics on a different girl. If she does smile, however, he takes her place and she sits in the middle of the circle and starts the game again.

Variation: Play "Make Me Laugh." The set up is the same as in "I love you honey, but I just can't smile," with one exception: instead of making the chosen person smile, the person in the center must make him laugh and can only do so by laughing himself.

Jungle Volleyball

Jungle volleyball is a game that mixes rules from both volleyball and racquetball. It accommodates large groups of people, and is best played indoors in a gym. The following rules make this game unique from either volleyball or racquetball:

1) There are no out of bounds.
2) As in racquetball, players benefit from using ceilings, corners, and walls as strategic targets.
3) Either team can hit the ball as many times as is necessary to get the ball over the net.
4) The ball can hit the ground once in between each hit from players on the same team. If the ball bounces on the ground twice in a row before a team member touches it, the opposing team wins the volley.
5) If the ball is caught in the net during a serve, another player may hit the ball to help it over the net.

Scoring is the same as in regular volleyball: the first team to score 15 points wins. The winning team must win by at least two points.

Kick The Can

For this group date, you need an aluminum can and an area where there are plenty of hiding places. One couple (the guardians) sits by the can, closes their eyes, and counts to sixty while the other couples hide. After the count of sixty, the couple guarding the can has to try to find the other couples without allowing anyone to reach the can and kick it. If someone kicks the can, anyone previously captured is free.

To capture another couple, one of the guardians must spot them, identify them by name by yelling, "Over the can on (names of the couple)!", and jump over the can. The couple that has been spotted and identified can save themselves by kicking the can before one of the guards jumps over it. Each couple must stay together except the couple guarding the can. The game is over when the guardians have captured every couple or when every couple is freed.

Kissing Buffalo

Feel like kissing a hairy bovine? If you answered yes, you'll need to go to a zoo because this activity isn't exactly what it appears to be. Kissing buffalo is a flirtatious activity involving a large group of people. Therefore, it's best to plan this as a huge, unattached group date.

To set up, divide everyone into two groups, one on each end of a large grassy area. These groups are buffalo herds. Select a boy and a girl from the groups to stand in between the two herds of buffalo. These two are wolves.

To play, the wolves yell, "Buffalo!" At this cue, the two herds stampede toward each other and the awaiting wolves, with the goal of safely reaching the opposite side. In the midst of the stampede, the wolves attempt to catch an opposite sex buffalo by kissing him or her on the cheek. When the stampede is over, all the kissed buffalo magically turn into wolves. Play continues until no buffalo are left. After the last buffalo is kissed, play again (of course).

Kissing Rugby

Keen ears and quick lips are needed for this large group date. Before the date prepare three sets of numbers in accordance with how many people are playing. For example, if ten boys and ten girls are playing, number pink slips of paper one through ten, blue slips of paper one through ten, and white slips of papers one through ten. Put the white set in a hat and mix them up. Give a blue number to each boy and a pink number to each girl. All of the participants sit in a circle, facing inward. Choose a boy and a girl to be kissed. We'll call them the "kiss-ees." The kiss-ees go to the middle of the circle and sit back to back. The white pieces of paper in the hat are given to them. Make sure that the circle is wide enough so that there is about ten feet between the kissers and the kiss-ees.

To play, one of the kiss-ees draws a number from the hat and yells it to the members of the circle. The boy and the girl with that number race to the kiss-ees. To win, the girl kisser must kiss the boy kiss-ee on the cheek before the boy kisser kisses the girl kiss-ee on the cheek, or vice-versa. The fastest kisser retains her number and takes her place again in the circle. The slower kisser, however, trades his number with the kiss-ee of the same sex, and replaces him in the middle of the circle while the kiss-ee he replaced finds a seat in the circle.

Lifesaver Pass

For this flirtatious event, you will need a package of Lifesavers candy and a box of toothpicks. Divide the participants into two teams. Line up the members of each team, alternating boy and girl. Give everyone a toothpick and instruct them to hold it between their teeth, pointing it straight forward like a spear. Give the first person in each line a Lifesaver.

At the "Go" signal, the first person in each row slides the Lifesaver onto his toothpick and passes it to the girl next to him. This is accomplished by maneuvering both toothpicks into the hole of the Lifesaver and sliding it from the first toothpick to the second toothpick. Continue in this manner until the Lifesaver reaches the last person in line. Absolutely no hands allowed! If the Lifesaver is dropped, it must be taken to the beginning person again, and the team must start over.

For greater action, have each team pass an entire pack of Lifesavers, one at a time. If a Lifesaver falls to the floor, it must be left there. The team that successfully passes the greatest number of Lifesavers to the end of its row in a given amount of time wins.

Variation: Do an orange pass. The setup is the same as the Lifesaver pass, except an orange is passed underneath the participants' chins. Each person must hold the orange between his chin and chest and pass it to the next person, who grabs it between his chin and chest. Play proceeds as in the Lifesaver pass.

Mingle-Mingle

Mingle-Mingle is a great way to start a party or other activity where some people might not know each other. To play, each person crosses his arms across his chest and smashes into a human conglomerate. When the host says, "Mingle-Mingle," each person spins in a circle saying "Mingle-Mingle," creating a confusing mass of bumping bodies. The host then shouts out a number (for example, "Seven!"). At this cue, the mingling stops and the group links arms into groups of seven. Each group sits down when the correct number is acquired. Anyone not in a group of seven before all the groups sit down is out, and the game continues until only two people are left. They are declared the winners.

Murder In The Dark

For this group date, the more couples that participate, the more fun the game will be. First, select a location that is large enough for everyone to sit in a circle, holding hands. When everyone arrives and is seated, dim the lights and put into a hat as many small pieces of paper as there are people in the circle. Mark one piece of paper with an "X." Instruct each person in the circle to take a piece of paper from the hat. The person who takes the "X" will be the secret murderer for that game.

The object of the game is for the murderer to "kill" everyone else in the circle without being detected. The murderer "kills" people by squeezing hands. If he wants to kill the person sitting five people to his left, he squeezes five times the person's hand on his left. The person on the left would subtract one squeeze and pass four squeezes to the person on his left. This continues until someone's hand is squeezed only once. When this occurs, he has been murdered. He should make a dramatic death sound, pull out of the circle, and let the hands re-connect without him.

If someone suspects a possible murderer, she makes an accusation by declaring who she thinks the murderer is. If another member of the circle seconds her motion, the accused must declare whether he is the murderer or not. If her accusation is correct, she wins the game. If she is wrong, however, she and the person that seconded her are dead.

The game is over when the true murderer's identity has been revealed or when everyone in the circle except the murderer is dead. When the game is over, simply put the papers back in the hat and play again.

Variation: Add additional challenge to this game by playing "Double Murder In The Dark." The rules are the same except there are two murderers who try to kill each other as well as everyone else in the group.

Ring on a String

Quick hands and sharp eyes are valuable for this activity. Form the participants into a circle, standing or sitting, all facing inward. To begin, thread a very long string through a ring and tie the ends of the string together, forming a circle along which the ring can slide freely. The participants each grab hold of the string with both hands. Send a person to the middle of the circle to count to ten with eyes closed while the ring is passed around the string. At the end of ten seconds, the middle person opens his eyes and tries to guess who in the circle has the ring. As he guesses, however, the ring is secretly being passed from hand to hand around the circle when the middle person is not looking. Keep track of how many guesses it takes before he locates the ring. Whoever gets caught with the ring is sent to the middle of the circle for the next round.

Sardines

This group date is similar to the game, "Hide and Seek." All you need to play is a large area where there is room for lots of people to hide. Select one couple to be "it." Whoever is "it" has sixty seconds to find a good hiding place big enough for two people. After the count of sixty seconds, all the remaining couples silently search for the hiding couple.

When a couple finds the hiding couple, it squashes into the hiding place with them, like sardines in a can. The game is over when all of the couples have found the group and are all crammed into the hiding place with them. The couple who finds the hiding couple first is "it" for the next game. If you want to make things more competitive, time each game. Whichever couple goes undiscovered for the longest period of time wins.

Shoe Scramble

This activity is a great way for people to learn more about each other while having fun. Have each person remove his or her shoes and throw them in a pile on the floor. Scramble the shoes into a thoroughly mixed-up pile. At a given signal, the participants grab any two shoes from the pile. They must locate the owner of each shoe and ask her two questions about herself. When the owner has answered the questions, she gets her shoe back. Continue until everyone has obtained their own shoes.

Three-Legged Soccer

This sport is just what it says it is. Divide the participants into two equal teams. Pair up the participants of each team into couples. Tie their inner legs together at the ankles and knees, forming several three-legged couples. Play soccer.

Train Tag

Have you ever tried touching a moving train? Neither have I, but for this game you'll become a moving train. Nominate a person to be the engine. The engine tries to add to his train by tagging another player. When a player is tagged, he connects to the engine by placing his hands on the engine's waist. The two now try to catch someone else to lengthen the train. However, when four people are caught, the third person becomes an engine and the train splits into two sets of two, with each train chasing the single players. Play continues until all but one person is caught. He is declared the winner, and becomes the first engine for the next round.

Variation: Make the tagging a little more difficult by making the rule that the train must always be connected boy-girl.

Who Am I?

On several index cards, write the names of famous people or characters, such as George Washington, Mother Goose, Miss Piggy, and Betsy Ross. Pin or tape one of these names on the back of each person. Everyone must find out who he or she is by asking questions to other members of the group that can be answered with only a "yes" or "no" answer, with a limit of two questions per person. The game continues until each person knows who he or she is. An award could be given to the person who figures out who he is most quickly.

Variation: Write action phrases on sticky labels, such as "Ignore Me," "Doubt Me," or "Smile at Me." Stick a label on the forehead of each person. When everyone has a label, tell them to socialize with each other. As they do so, they should read the labels on the other people's foreheads and act towards them accordingly. The object is for each person to figure out what action phrase is written on his own forehead by the reactions of others to him.

Winkums

Winkums is a fast-moving, action-packed game that requires at least ten people to play. About twenty people would be ideal. To set up, choose a soft area to play on, such as grass or padded carpet, and then divide by gender into two groups. Call the group of girls the guardians and the group of boys the captives. There must be one more guardian than captive.

Each guardian, except the lonely guardian, selects a captive to guard. The object of the game is for the lonely guardian to steal another guardian's captive. To play, the captives kneel down in a large circle facing inward. Each of the guardians except the lonely guardian stands closely behind her captive. The lonely guardian also stands in the circle, but without a captive in front of her.

Each captive boy watches the lonely guardian's eyes closely. The other guardians, however, must keep their eyes on their captives. The lonely guardian selects a desired captive and winks at him. He must then attempt to dash across the circle and touch her feet. His guardian must attempt to stop him before he reaches her. Tackling is usually in order. If he doesn't make it across the circle, the defending guardian retains him as her captive and the lonely guardian winks at another. If he reaches her, however, he becomes her captive and the guardian he escaped from becomes the new lonely guardian. After several rounds, switch roles so that the girls are the captives and the boys are the guardians.

White Elephant Party

Invite a large group of friends over for a White Elephant party. A White Elephant gift is either a joke gift or a gift which is of little value to you but which might be of value to someone else. The funnier they are, the better.

Ask each person invited to bring a wrapped White Elephant gift to the party. Sit in a large circle, facing inward. Place all of the White Elephant gifts in the middle of the circle. Make a slip of paper for each person. If thirty people are present, number the papers one through thirty. Put the numbers in a hat and have each person randomly choose one.

When everyone has a number, person number one chooses a gift from the center of the circle and opens it. Person number two can either choose person number one's gift or a wrapped gift from the center of the circle instead. If he chooses to take person number one's gift, person number one then selects a new gift from the center of the circle and opens it. Person number three then can either take any opened gift in the circle or a wrapped gift from the middle of the circle. Play continues in this manner until everyone has a gift.

Chapter Two

Group Dates

Advertising Agents

For this date, obtain several household products such as liquid soap, a can of hair spray, and a box of cereal. Lay them on a table (this works best if you have at least one product for each couple involved). Assign each product a number; then label several slips of paper with corresponding numbers and put them in a hat.

Have each couple choose a number out of the hat and find its corresponding household product. For the next thirty minutes, each couple will prepare an advertisement for their chosen product. The advertisement could be a dialogue, a skit, a song, or a combination of these. After thirty minutes, take turns presenting your advertisements to the other couples. Then vote on which product you would be most tempted to buy after viewing its advertisement.

Alphabet Road Rally

Select a home base from which everyone will begin. Each couple is a team in a race and competes against the other couples. The object is for each couple to obtain 26 objects, each beginning with a different letter of the alphabet, within a one-hour time frame. Do this by going door to door within a designated area and asking people for them. At the end of the hour, have everyone meet back at home base and compare the objects you collected.

Variation: To make this more difficult, make a rule that each of the objects must be obtained in alphabetical order, with the A object first and the Z object last.

Ancestral Potluck Dinner

This date differs from the traditional potluck dinner, which requires that everyone attending the date must bring a dish of food. Each couple must prepare and bring an inexpensive type of food from a country where some of his or her ancestors were born. For example, if you have German ancestors, you and your date might prepare and bring German pancakes.

Barter For Bigger And Better

For this group date, give each couple a small, monetarily worthless object such a pebble, with which you will race against each other to barter for something either bigger or better. Select a home base from which to begin. In a one-hour time period, each couple must take its pebble to a stranger and trade it for something either bigger in size or better in monetary value. After the hour is up, the couples return to home base to select the two winning couples. The couple returning with the biggest item wins the first category and the couple who returns with the object of most monetary value wins the second category.

Beach Art

Prior to this date, each couple should pitch in a dollar to purchase a package of plaster of Paris (generally available at craft and hardware stores). Along with the plaster of Paris and a small bucket, meet everyone at a sandy beach near a lake, river, or ocean.

Draw a design together in the wet sand with your fingers. Then make a mold of the design by digging out the sand at least two inches deep, smoothing the bottom of the design. Mix the plaster of Paris according to the directions on the package and pour it into your design. Add sea shells or rocks to the design if you desire. After the mold has set, dig it out of the sand.

For a twist to this date, make molds of your faces. Close your eyes, hold your breath, and press your face into a pile of fresh, wet sand. Pour the plaster of Paris into the face mold. Write a dedication on it before it dries to remember the date by.

Bridge Building

For this date, have each couple contribute a dollar to purchase two bridge-building kits from a craft store. Divide the group into teams and give each team one of the kits. Awards could be given for the bridge which holds the most weight or has the most creative design. Make sure rules are set for the competition beforehand. For example, each bridge must be no taller than seven inches and must have at least three base blocks.

Broom Ice-hockey

Locate a free public ice skating rink, such as a frozen lake or pond. The Parks and Recreation information center in your area may have suggestions for facilities as well as necessary information about ice conditions. Before the date, go to your designated lake and sweep off any snow to make a playing field of ice. Afterward, make a goal out of snow on each end of the playing field. Have everyone pick up their dates, making sure that they are dressed warmly. Each person will need a broom.

After arriving at the playing field, divide the couples into two equal teams and play broom ice-hockey, using a tennis ball for the puck and brooms for hockey sticks. Bring thermos full of hot chocolate to help keep warm.

Variation: Play broom hockey in an empty parking lot or gym using a broom and a tennis ball or baseball as the puck.

Campfire Stories

Instead of sitting around a campfire trying to scare the "bejeebers" out of each other by telling ghost stories, try telling pioneer stories and spiritual experiences instead. The best experiences are often from your own ancestry or in pioneer journals.

Candy Treasure Hunt

For this group date, each couple takes a dollar and hunts around town for an hour purchasing as many wrapped candies as possible. When time is up, meet back at your house to count candies to determine the winning couple.

Cardboard Car Drive-in

This drive-in movie group date will work even if you don't have a car, because you will be making your own cars as part of the date. Have everyone in your group meet for the date at your house where you have previously collected supplies such as large cardboard boxes, magic markers, construction paper, and flashlights. Each couple must make its car out of cardboard. Afterwards, everyone "drives" their cars into the living room. Have someone judge the cars to select a winning couple. The winners have to pop popcorn for the others. When the popcorn is ready, put in a video and enjoy the show.

Charades

Ready for an evening of laughter? This is a great way to laugh until you cry. To play, have someone not involved in the date write several words or phrases on slips of paper. Tell them the nature of the activity so that they can write words and phrases that will be fun and challenging to act out. Put the slips of paper into a hat. Each couple takes turns choosing a slip of paper from the hat, brainstorming together for sixty seconds, and silently acting out their word or phrase while everyone else tries to guess what it is.

Coded Dinner

Invite a few couples over for dinner at your home. Assign each couple to bring a specific type of food. Before the date, make a menu for each person in the group. These menus should offer several different foods, each written in code form. (For example: "Italian worms" = spaghetti; "chopped heads" = salad; "pronghorn" = fork; "vase" = cup.) When everyone arrives, seat them and offer them their menus. Have everyone order by code, and then serve them whatever they ordered. Depending on the order, you or your date could end up with all food and no silverware, or all silverware and no food!

Come As You Are Date

Before this date, the guys need to get together with everyone who plans to bring someone to this date and plan an inexpensive breakfast to be held at your house. Have everyone call his date's parents and ask them if they could get his date out of bed at 6:30 a.m. on a certain morning. On the morning of the date, have everyone go to their dates' homes, have their parents wake their dates up, give them thirty seconds to throw on some slippers, and take them to your house for breakfast. Make sure that the rest of you are dressed only thirty seconds out of bed as well. After everyone has arrived, serve breakfast.

Couple's Contest

For this double date, you will need a friend or parent to help you set up by developing a scavenger hunt and hiding the clues. Each couple is a team and competes against the other couple in several events. As couples you will drive different cars but never separate during the hunt. You will compete by using a point system to determine the winning team. At the end of the scavenger hunt, the couple with the most points wins. Example:

Clue #1: The first clue sends you to a church meetinghouse where two sets of scriptures are waiting for you, hidden beneath a tree. Inside the scriptures is an envelope which gives you instructions to scripture chase to find 2 Corinthians 13:12. Whichever team finds and reads the scripture first receives one point. Also inside the envelope is another envelope which contains clue number two, paper, a pencil to keep track of the score, and a one dollar bill for each couple.

Clue #2: The second clue takes you to Taco Bell, where you are to ask for the order which was previously placed in your name. After paying for the order with your dollar bills, you are each given a bean burrito, a blindfold, and another envelope. Inside the envelope are instructions to blindfold your date and feed each other your bean burritos, as well as another envelope for clue number three. The team that successfully eats their burritos first scores one point. Then open the envelope for clue number three.

Clue #3: The third clue sends you to a tennis court where you find a tennis ball and instructions to play doubles tennis without racquets. You also find another envelope containing clue number four. The team that wins two out of three volleys scores one point. Open clue number four.

Clue #4: Clue number four sends you to a gas station. Here, the gas station attendant gives you two long, skinny balloons, an envelope containing clue number five, and instructions. You are to blow up the balloons to full capacity, then tie them off. Then, you must all race to pop your balloons using any part of your bodies except your hands, feet, or bottoms. The couple who pop their balloon first receives one point. Open clue number five.

Clue #5: The last clue takes you to a park, where you will find instructions underneath the slide. Here, you are instructed to slide down the slide and then race back to your house, obeying all traffic rules. Whoever rings the doorbell first wins the last point.

Cultural Progressive Dinner

This group date will add cultural flavor to the traditional progressive dinner, which consists of eating an appetizer at one person's house, the main dish at another person's house, and the dessert at a last person's house. Before the date, contact the couples who will be attending to plan an inexpensive dinner menu with food from different countries. Have each couple use a dollar to purchase ingredients for one course of the meal, to be prepared beforehand and then served to everyone else.

The date could go something like this: Meet everyone at the first house, "China," to begin the progressive dinner. Here you will all eat an appetizer of won ton soup. Then the group goes to the next house, "Mexico." Eat a main dish of bean burritos here. Finally, go to the last house, "England," and eat truffles for dessert.

Variation: Have a campfire progressive dinner. Each couple must make its own fire and cook a different part of the meal over it.

Variation: Have a regressive dinner, in which dessert is served first, then the main course, and finally the appetizer.

Dictionary Date

For this group date, paper and pencil are needed for each person, as well as a dictionary, and a great imagination. The game is played by having one person look up a word in the dictionary that nobody knows. He tells everyone the word, and everyone writes down the most believable definitions they can make up for that word. Then, everyone turns their definitions in to the person who picked the word. Meanwhile, he writes the true definition on his piece of paper. When the definitions are turned in, the person who chose the word reads all of the definitions aloud, and each player must select the definition he thinks is correct. Everyone casts their votes secretly, so no one influences the others' decisions.

Scoring: If the correct dictionary definition is not chosen, the person who chose the word gets one point. If you chose the correct definition, you receive one point. Anyone whose made-up definition gets chosen by someone else receives one point for each person he fooled. After the first round, the dictionary rotates one player to the left, and that player selects the next word.

Disney Night

What better way is there to thank the Walt Disney company for wholesome entertainment than to have a Disney night? Have each couple bring their favorite Walt Disney movie, any Disney memorabilia they have, and a snack. Between movies, talk about your favorite Disneyland or Disneyworld rides or your most recent trip there.

Double Date With Parents

Although there's really no such thing as a free lunch, this date comes pretty close. Invite your parents on a double date on the following condition: you and your date will cook the meal if your parents will provide the ingredients.

Downtown Foot Rally

For this group date, those participating will learn more about your neighborhood. Ideally, the person who sets up the rally beforehand will not participate in the race, but he can come along if he doesn't disclose any of the answers. This person should walk through the neighborhood creating a list of facts learned while walking around town, such as:

1. How many stickers are there in the window of the paint store?
2. What is the highest mailbox number in the post office?
3. How many pumps does the gas station have?
4. What is the most popular video rented this year according to the video store?
5. How much does it cost to rent a bicycle at the sporting goods store?

For the date, the couples meet at a starting point and are given a list of these questions. They will find the answers to these questions by going to the locations mentioned on the list. The goal of the rally is for each couple to answer as many questions as they can, and then return to the starting place.

When the couples return to the starting place, score all the couple's answers. Each correct answer is worth one point. The first couple back receives an additional point for speed.

Drive-in Movie

Some drive-in movie theaters offer carload specials, such as five dollars a carload. Plan a big group date. Have everyone meet outside the drive-in theater entrance and get into the back of a pickup truck with lawn chairs and bean bags to sit on. Chip in your money for the admission and enjoy the show.

Egg Racing

This event definitely won't take the whole evening,

but it's a fun thing to do while you're waiting for other couples to show up or when you have run out of things to do but don't want to go home yet. It's quick, simple, and amusing.

Declare a starting line and a finish line on a linoleum floor (this doesn't work well on carpet). Give each contestant an egg and a spoon. When you say go, the contestants race toward the finish line, pushing their eggs with only their spoons. The winner should feel "eggstra" special.

Variation: Using a yardstick, race potatoes across the lawn outside.

Fashion Show

Plan a fashion show at your house. Invite several couples and their parents to attend. Tell each couple to sneak some of their parents' old outfits out of the attic or wherever they hide them. For the fashion show, in front of the parents, model their old clothes to the music of their era.

Variation: Have a celebrity look-alike fashion show. See which couple can dress up to look the most like celebrities. Give a small award to the winning couple.

Variation: Have a fashion show at the mall. Have each person try on three or four different outfits per store and model them for each other.

Field Trip

For this educational group date, tour an interesting facility in your area such as a power plant, a fruit-packing plant, a saw mill, an automobile manufacturing plant, a fish hatchery, a military base, government headquarters, or an aviation center. Before the date, telephone the facility to receive its permission and to set up a free tour.

Find Your Picnic

This double date has two parts. Each couple sets up a scavenger hunt for the other couple by taking thirty minutes to hide the following items from a typical table setting: plastic forks, knives, spoons, plates, cups, and paper napkins, which are all hidden within a designated area. Each couple then creates clues to help the other couple find the hidden items. For the second part of the date, both couples meet back at the starting point, exchange clues, and race to find all of the hidden items. After the items have been found, meet back at the starting point and eat an inexpensive picnic on the table settings you find.

Finger Paint Pictionary

This group date is played just like normal Pictionary, except you use finger paints and butcher paper instead of pencil and paper to draw the pictures. Hang the completed paintings on the wall to dry and to display your creative art gallery. Each couple can pitch in a dollar to buy a set of finger paints, or a simple batch of homemade finger paints can be made by adding food coloring to either toothpaste or hand lotion.

Variation: To make this game a fun and edible mess, make a batch of pudding and use it instead of finger paints. When you're finished drawing, just lick your fingers clean.

Variation: Play modeling-dough Pictionary. For this variation, instead of drawing pictures, you must shape objects out of modeling dough for your teammate to guess. A simple recipe to make homemade modeling dough: combine 1 cup flour, 1 cup water, 1 tablespoon oil, 1/2 cup salt, 1 teaspoon cream of tartar, and food coloring in a pan. Cook over medium heat until mixture pulls away from sides of the pan and becomes doughy in consistency. Knead until cool. This recipe keeps for three months unrefrigerated.

Frisbee Football/Rugby

This group date is played just like regular football except you use a frisbee instead of a football. You can play a faster paced game by turning it into frisbee rugby. Do this by throwing the frisbee to others on your team but surrendering it to the other team if it ever hits the ground.

Garage Semi-Formal

Ask your date to a semi-formal dance when no organized dance is being held, and have your friends do the same. Before the date, clean and decorate your garage and set up a stereo inside. Invite the couples to your garage, turn on the music, and dance the night away.

Gotcha

For this group date, each couple will need either a squirt-gun or a squirt-bottle. Meet together inside a large building such as a warehouse or a school building, or play outdoors on either a farm or a forested area. Divide into teams. The goal is to squirt members of the other team but to avoid getting squirted by them.

Hamburger Hunt

Each couple should provide two hamburger buns and

two patties and meet at your house. After they arrive, make a list of the ingredients all would like to put on the hamburgers. Then, divide the list between couples and have everyone scavenger hunt to obtain the items on their lists. When everyone is back with the ingredients, barbecue the hamburgers.

Hide and Seek In The Dark

This nocturnal group date is best played in a basement or other dark area of a house. Use a room that is pitch black when the lights are turned off. A minimum of six people are needed to play. Select a person to be the seeker. The seeker leaves the darkened room and counts to sixty while the others hide.

The object of the game is for the seeker to enter the dark room and then find and correctly identify one of the hiders. Once the seeker has found a person, however, he can only try to identify them by touching their hands and face. No talking is allowed by the hider. To avoid being properly detected, the hiders can exchange jewelry, hats, rings, or glasses (don't worry, they don't help much in the dark anyway) before the seeker enters the room.

After gathering as many clues as possible, the seeker announces who she thinks she has found. If she is correct, the person found becomes the new seeker. If she is wrong, she must be the seeker for the next round.

Variation: Play Hide and Seek outside in the dark. Give the seeker a flashlight to find the hiding couples.

Hide and Spy

This group date works well at a shopping mall or large store. Meet the other couples at a designated place and time in the mall. Each couple will need paper, a pencil, and a watch. To play the game, give each couple five minutes to hide together from everyone else.

After everyone is hidden, the spying begins. Each couple secretly tries to find the other couples without being spotted themselves. When you find another couple, write down the time and location you saw them. The object of the game is to spy out the other couples, and to be the first couple back to the designated starting point, but avoid being spied by the other couples during the search.

Homemade Movies

For this group date, you will watch a movie but the movie has to be made first. With all of the couples together, write a script for a short movie in which you are the actors and actresses. Assign roles, find and dress in simple costumes, choose filming locations and then, using a home video camera, go to the selected locations and make your movie. When you're finished filming, return to your house, make popcorn, and watch the movie together.

Hot Seats

This group activity is not only fun but is educational for all couples involved, whether they have just starting dating or have been dating for some time. A minimum of three couples should participate. To set up the activity, place two chairs back to back in the middle of a room. Seat a couple in these "hot seats" as the first contestants. The other couples find seats around the edges of the room. They are the questioners.

To play, the questioners count in unison to three. On the count of three, the contestants each turn their heads either to the right or to the left. If they turn their heads in opposite directions, the boy will answer a question from one of the questioners; if they turn their heads in the same direction, the girl will answer the question. One of the questioners then asks a question to the appropriate member of the couple such as, "What is your date's favorite flavor of ice cream?"

If the boy must answer the question, then the girl writes the correct answer to the question on a piece of paper. The boy then announces the answer (or what he thinks to be the answer) to the group. If he is correct, the couple scores a point. If he is incorrect, no point is given. Play continues until the couple has been asked ten questions, after which they trade places with another couple, who are asked ten new questions in the same manner. The game is over after every couple has had a turn in the "hot seats." The couple with the most points at the end of the game wins.

Human Bowling

Make your own bowling alley and then be the bowling balls! To make the lane, lay a long, narrow tarp on some grass outside and cover it with water. At the end of the lane, set up either a plastic set of bowling pins or several plastic cups in bowling-pin formation. To bowl, take turns sliding across the wet tarp into the pins, knocking down as many as possible. Keep score as in regular bowling. You could have a water fight to clean up.

Inner-Tube River Race

Borrow inner tubes or a small raft and drive to a nearby stream. As you travel up the stream, indicate a finish line and leave some towels there. Then travel as far up the stream as you want to race. Set the necessary rules for the race before you begin. When each couple is on its inner tube, yell, "GO!" and race to the finish line.

Make sure your date knows the nature of this activity beforehand so that he or she can dress appropriately. Also, use caution in selecting a stream that is safe and is not too rapid for this type of activity.

It Happened To Me

For this revealing group date, each participant writes down one of his most embarrassing moments on a piece of paper. Below the experience, he writes the names of two other people in the group along with his own name, in random order. Then, all the papers are placed in a hat and mixed up.

Three people will claim ownership to each embarrassing experience. The object of the game is for the participants to determine which person actually had the experience and which two people are bluffing. To do this, draw one of the slips of paper out of the hat and read the embarrassing moment aloud. When the laughing ceases, read the names of the three names that appear below the experience. Each of these people then must relate the circumstances surrounding the embarrassing moment. The one to whom the experience really happened must tell the truth, while the other two will relate made-up circumstances to try to fool the others.

After the three stories have been presented, the rest of the participants vote on who they believe the experience actually happened to. When everyone has voted, the real embarrassed person steps forth.

Knock and Run

Experience the thrill of trying to escape without being caught after leaving a nice surprise at someone's doorstep. Sneak up to the doors of friends and leave a nice note or a plate of cookies. Ring the doorbell and sprint for cover.

Lady Luck and a Chocolate Bar

For this group date, buy the biggest chocolate bar you can afford to purchase with your dollar. Set the candy on a table along with a pair of dice, a fork, and a knife. Also, place on the table some clothing accessories such as a scarf, gloves, glasses, a hat, and a belt. Gather everyone in a circle around the table.

The object of this game is for each player to individually eat as much of the chocolate bar as possible. To play, participants take turns rolling the dice onto the table, attempting to roll doubles or a seven. When one gets lucky, he immediately attempts to put on all of the accessories as quickly as he can.

When fully dressed in the accessories, the lucky person eats as much of the chocolate bar as possible. No fingers allowed! It must be touched with only the fork and knife. The dice continue to roll. As soon as someone else rolls a seven or doubles, they strip the first lucky person of the accessories and attempt to dress and eat the chocolate bar themselves and so forth.

Library Scavenger Hunt

Before this group date, create a list of questions for which the answers can be found by looking in books in a public library. These questions can ask for historical dates, geographical locations, or publisher information, for example. Give each participating couple a list of questions to answer. Then, in silence, race to answer all of the questions on your lists. The winning couple receives a bookmark.

Variation: See who can find the oldest book in the library within a designated time period (no using computers).

Line Dancing

If you're in a heel kickin', boot slappin' mood, then this date is for you. Find a person that knows how to line-dance and ask him or her to teach you and your group how to line-dance to country music.

Moonlight Volleyball

Go to a park, a beach, or to anyplace where you can play volleyball. Divide into two teams and play volleyball by the light of the moon. You may want to use a fluorescent volleyball if you have one, since they tend to be more visible in the dark.

Mud Football

For this group date, find a dusty place where you can play football. Just add water and you'll have the ingredients for a perfect mud football game. After the game, have a water fight to wash off.

Variation: Play mud volleyball instead.

Museum Hunt

This group date takes place in a museum that can be toured free of admission. Give each couple paper and a pencil. The couples have thirty minutes to freely tour the museum. As they tour, have them find fifteen interesting facts obtained from the written information located on the displays, and create fifteen quiz questions from the facts they obtained.

When the thirty minutes are over, the couples meet back together and exchange questions. They then have one hour to find as many answers to their lists of questions as possible. Be careful to be respectful of the other people touring the museum.

Music Videos

Dress in trendy clothes, play some music, assign someone to operate a video camera, and record your own music videos. If you don't have the instruments you need, just make them out of cardboard beforehand.

Object Scavenger Hunt

For this group date, give each couple a list of 25 items that they must race to acquire within one hour. Whoever returns first with all of the items or who has the most items when the time limit is up wins the game.

Old Doll Overhaul

Each person brings either an old doll, an old stuffed animal, or an old toy to your house for this date. Clean the old toys up as well as you can, repairing any broken parts if possible. After fixing them up, donate them to a local charity.

Olympics

This group date will turn your home into an olympic arena where teams from "all over the world" will come to compete for gold, silver, and bronze medals. Assign each couple to represent a foreign country and have them dress accordingly.

Before the competition begins, allow each team to introduce itself and tell a little about the country they represent. After the opening ceremony, the athletes will compete in events which are set up in different areas of your home. The events of this competition are limited only by your imagination. Following is a list of possible events:

1. Miniature Golf: Place paper or plastic cups strategically throughout your home for holes. Competitors must knock a golf ball into a cup (which is lying on its side) with a putter.
2. Bowling: Set up paper cups in bowling pin formation and use a tennis ball for a bowling ball. Mark the edges of the bowling lane with masking tape.
3. High Jump: Hang marshmallows from the ceiling on a string. The athlete must jump up and pull the marshmallow off the string, using only his mouth. If he succeeds, raise the marshmallow an inch higher for his next jump.
4. Long Jump: Have the couple stand side by side and tie their inside ankles together. Let them jump as far as they can in one leap.
5. Javelin: Give the contestants straws and see how far they can throw them.
6. Discus: Contestants are given paper plates and see how far they can throw them.
7. The 10-foot Dash: With pieces of masking tape, mark off ten feet from start to finish. Then, race to the finish line while pushing a penny with your nose.

8. The 25-foot Hurdles: Mark off 25 feet from start to finish and place paper cups in a line across the lane every five feet. The team of athletes must run this race together on hands and knees, one in front of the other, with the athlete in back holding on to the ankles of the one in front. They must successfully cross the hurdles, adding five seconds to their time for each paper cup knocked over.

Out-of-Season Party

Invite several couples to a party in which they must dress in clothing which is not generally worn during the current season. Prepare and participate in activities around this theme. For example, play a short game of tennis wearing snowmobile suits or build a snowman wearing shorts and t-shirts.

Pancake Party

Invite a few couples over for breakfast. Have a contest to see who can make the most recognizable animal-shaped pancakes. You could also have a contest to see who could eat the most pancakes.

Perfect Pizza Party

Invite several couples to a pizza-making party. Have each couple bring an ingredient for the pizza. As you create the pizza make things challenging by imposing some restrictions. For example, blindfold one couple and instruct them to make the pizza dough, and tie the hands of another couple and have them cut up the peppers and onions. When your perfect pizza is assembled, put it in the oven to cook, and then eat and enjoy.

Pig Dinner

Make your favorite messy pasta and invite a few brave couples over for dinner. Have a "pig dinner" together where no one gets to use either their hands or their silverware to eat dinner.

Pinata Party

Get together with a few other couples to make a pinata. Instructions for making a pinata: Blow up a balloon. Tear newspaper into long, thin strips and dip the strips into a runny paste of flour and water. Smooth the strips onto the balloon. Cover the entire balloon with two or three layers of pasty strips. Allow the pinata to dry for a few hours outside, or dry it yourself with a blow dryer.

When the newspaper is dry, decorate the pinata with crepe paper and glue. Then pop the balloon inside by pushing a pin through the hardened pinata. Cut a two-inch hole at the top and fill your pinata with candy or other treats.

When your pinata is finished, hang it from a basketball standard outside and take turns trying to break it by swinging at it with a baseball bat while blindfolded.

Puzzle Party

For this group date, have each couple bring a puzzle to your house. Pop some popcorn, buy some soda, exchange puzzles with another couple, and have a contest to see who can put their puzzle together the fastest. Make sure each puzzle has the same number of pieces.

Quarters Maze

This date will require a group of people, at least two vehicles, and a quarter for each vehicle. Select a starting point and an ending point in your neighborhood. Divide the couples into cars, drive to the starting point, and begin.

Each car begins driving away from the starting point. As the vehicle approaches an intersection, someone in the car must flip the quarter. If the quarter comes up heads, the driver must turn left at the intersection. If the quarter comes up tails, the driver must turn right at the intersection.

The object of the game is to be the first vehicle to reach the ending point before a designated time period, while obeying all game and traffic rules. When time has expired, if your car has not reached the ending point, write down the time and your exact location, and then drive to the ending point without following the quarters rule. The first vehicle to reach the ending point before time expires is declared the winner. If none of the vehicles reached the ending point before time expired, the vehicle that was the nearest to the ending point when time was up is the winner.

Radio Road Dance

For this group date, invite your date to go dancing with you and have your friends do the same. Each couple should ride in a separate car. Drive the caravan of cars to an empty public parking lot. Park your cars in a circle with the headlights facing inward. Then, tune all of your radios to the same station, roll down the windows, turn the radios up, and dance in the lighted circle created by the cars.

Rainbow War

For this group date, have each person wear an old shirt that can get stained, bring a squirt bottle, and meet at a designated open field. Divide everyone into two teams. Put water mixed with red food coloring in one team's bottles and water mixed with blue in the other's. Set boundaries on the field, and have a rainbow war by hunting members of the other team down and squirting them on their old shirts with your color, thus eliminating them. The team with a player wearing the last unmarked shirt wins. Trade colors and play again.

To play with more than two teams, follow the same rules as above but add a new color for each team. To make this version more challenging, include the rule that a person must be squirted by at least two colors before being eliminated.

Record Setting

Most of us, at some time in our lives, have wanted to set a record in an event. Hopefully by the end of this date, that dream will be realized for many people in your group. To set records, compete with each other to determine which of you can outperform the others in certain events. Examples of events:

1. Marshmallow stuffing: see who can fit the most miniature marshmallows into his mouth without swallowing.
2. Bubble blowing: see who can blow the biggest bubble with a piece of bubble gum.
3. Largest lungs: see who can hold her breath the longest.
4. No pain no gain: see who can squeeze an ice cube for the longest amount of time.

San Francisco Supper

For this group date, invite everyone to your house

for a spaghetti dinner. Seat them at a table which is set with everything necessary to eat except silverware. Have each person choose a number out of a hat. Then, bring out a tray covered with several kitchen utensils such as potato mashers, wire whisks, tongs, and spatulas. Each utensil has a number on it. Help your guests find their utensils by matching their numbers to those on the utensils. The couples then put on huge bibs and eat their spaghetti dinners using their selected utensils.

Scribble Interpreting

Paper and a few crayons are all you will need for this crazy activity. A few couples sit in a circle, each person having a piece of paper and a crayon in front of them. Each person then thinks of an animal to draw on his paper, but doesn't tell anyone else which animal he has chosen. One at a time, each person closes his eyes and attempts to draw his animal on the paper without either touching his other hand to the paper or removing his crayon from the paper. His object must be drawn in one continuous line.

When the person is finished drawing, everyone else writes on a slip of paper which animal they think he has drawn. If someone is correct, she gets a point and the person who drew the picture gets a point as well. Play as many rounds as you desire. If you want to make this really difficult, have each couple decide on an animal together. They both then close their eyes, hold on to the crayon together, and attempt to draw the animal.

Scripture Treasure Hunt

For this group date, arrange a treasure hunt in which several couples follow scripture-related clues to find a treasure at the end of the hunt. For example, send them to the Garden of Eden (a neighbor's garden) or to the Tower of Babel (a tall building). End up at someone's home for refreshments.

Service Project Scavenger Hunt

Prior to this group date, make a list of simple services that could be provided to people in your neighborhood, such as mopping a floor, vacuuming a carpet, or washing some dishes. For the date, give each couple a copy of the list of services and race to see who can render the list of services first. Only one service can be given per household.

Silver Platter Pizza

For this group date, have either all the guys or all the girls get together previously and make a homemade pizza, pitching in each person's dollar to purchase the ingredients. Invite dates over to your house for a formal dinner. Set the table with your finest tablecloth, china, and candles. Make sure everyone knows to dress in formal wear. Seat everyone, bring out a covered silver platter, set it on the table, take the lid off, and reveal the homemade pizza.

Variation: Do a similar thing for breakfast using cold cereal.

Slap Cards

For this date, you will need a deck of colored playing cards. Deal the entire deck of cards out evenly to all players. Each person leaves her cards face down in a pile in front of her. To begin, the first person plays a card by putting it in the center of the table face up, revealing its color. Each successive participant plays in like manner until two cards of the same color are played consecutively. When this occurs, all players race to slap a certain part of their body, depending on which color was repeated.

For example, if two red cards are played, all players must slap their hearts. Green may represent thighs, yellow the stomach, and blue foreheads. The last player to slap the proper part of his body takes the center pile and adds it to the bottom of his deck. The first person to get rid of all his cards wins.

Snipe Hunting

[Note: Though snipes are only imaginary birds, going "snipe hunting" can be a lot of fun when you are with people who think that snipes really exist!] Tell your group you are going snipe hunting. Have everyone wear old clothes and bring a flashlight and a pillow case. With your group, go to a hill that is "teeming with snipes." Tell them what to be looking for during the hunt: a snipe is a bird that runs on the ground and feeds on worms and insects at night. They are delicious to eat and fun to catch. Tell your group that in order to catch a snipe, they need to scare them by making a lot of noise and then shine their flashlights into their pillow cases since when snipes are afraid, they have a tendency to run towards the light.

Have everyone who has been snipe hunting before (and is experienced in catching them) wait at the bottom of the hill with their pillow cases open and their flashlights shining into them. Have everyone else go to the top of the hill and make a lot of noise to scare the snipes down the hill and into the pillow cases. Although snipes are only imaginary creatures, it's amazing to see how many people think they actually see them on a snipe hunt. This date will provide lots of funny memories for you and your date as you remember how many snipes people "saw" and chased in the moonlight that night.

Snow Family

For this date each couple builds a snowman, each being a member of the Snow family. If there are several couples with you, make it a Snow family reunion. When you are finished, take some pictures of all of you standing with the Snow family.

Snow Football

This group date is best with at least four couples. Dress warmly, find an open, snow-covered area, stomp out the boundaries for a football field in the snow, divide into teams, and then play snow football.

Snow Sculpturing Contest

Invite several couples to a snow sculpturing contest. Select a theme such as animals, food, or forms of transportation. Then have each couple sculpt an object having to do with the theme. When you are finished, vote on the best sculpture and give a small award for the winners.

Snow Tag

Everyone knows that if you're outside and it's cold, a little exercise will warm you up. This is fun exercise. To begin the activity, stomp out a maze of inter-connecting trails in the snow. These trails are your game board, and all players must stay on the trails as they run through the snow. Play snow tag, selecting a couple to be "it." This couple must chase the other couples, attempting to tag them. When "it" tags a couple, that couple becomes the new "it" and play continues as before.

Sound Scavenger Hunt

For this group date, each couple needs a blank cassette tape and a tape recorder that runs on batteries. Give them a list of sounds that they have to record such as a cash register opening, a dog barking, a crosswalk beeping, or a toilet flushing. Race the other couples to see who can record the most sounds on its list within an allotted time period. When time is up, meet back at your house and listen to the sounds each couple has recorded.

Spider Maze

Are you one of those people that enjoys crossword puzzles, mazes, and word searches? If so, you should enjoy this "amazing" date.

Instead of doing a maze on paper, you'll get to walk through one. A non-participant sets up the maze by stringing several long strands of yarn through a grove of trees at about chest level. One end of each piece of yarn should be tied to a center tree and then should lead away from that tree in different directions. As each piece of yarn approaches another tree, it should be tied to that tree so that the yarn is tied to various trees throughout the grove. Only one piece of yarn should lead from the center tree out of the maze. The rest of the pieces of yarn should dead-end somewhere in the grove.

All couples begin at the center tree. They each select a piece of yarn from which to begin, and while holding on, race to see who can get through the maze the fastest without ever letting go of the yarn.

Sprinkler Kick Ball

Choose a yard that is big enough for a nice game of kick ball. Set up bases, make your rules, and then turn on the sprinklers and play. Be careful not to damage the sprinklers or yourselves and make sure you dress for wet.

Story Telling

For this group date, each person will need a piece of paper and a pencil. Instruct each person to write the beginning paragraph of a story on his or her piece of paper, developing it just enough to introduce the characters and basic setting. After two minutes, tell everyone to stop writing and to pass their pieces of paper one person to the right.

Have each person silently read the beginning paragraph of the newly-received story and then continue writing that story on the piece of paper. After two more minutes, pass the papers one person to the right again. Continue writing on and passing the papers until each person has written on each story and has received his or her own completed story back. Then, take turns reading the stories to each other.

Variation: Sit in a circle in a comfortable place. Have one person start a story by giving the opening sentence, such as: "Once upon a time, there was a pig." The story continues around the circle, with each person adding a sentence along the way.

Supermarket Sweep

Since this date takes place at a supermarket, obtain prior permission from the supermarket manager. Also, it's easier to do this later at night when the market is less crowded.

Each couple is a team and will need a shopping cart, a calculator, a pen, and paper. No money will be spent. The object of this activity is for each team to put as many items as possible, totaling less than ten dollars, into its shopping cart within a thirty-minute time period. No two items can be alike. At the end of thirty minutes, all teams meet at the front of the store and count the items in their carts to determine the winning team. Then, each couple switches carts with another couple and races to see which couple can put all of the items in the shopping cart back on the shelves in their proper places in the shortest amount of time.

Surprise Slide Show

For this group date, call your date's parents and ask them to let you borrow some baby pictures or slides of your date. Invite your friends to do the same. Then, ask your date over to watch a movie at your house. Meet there with all the other couples and show the slides and baby pictures of everyone's dates for the movie.

Synchronized Spaghetti Sucking

For this group date, invite a bunch of couples to your house for a spaghetti dinner. Seat everyone around a large table and serve everyone big plates of spaghetti. Synchronize the dinner by connecting everyone's hands with a tight string so that everyone has to lift their forks to their mouths at the same time in order to eat.

Table Sundae

For this group date, combine each couple's dollar and purchase a half-gallon of ice cream and a can of whipped cream. Additional toppings may be purchased according to the number of couples contributing dollars.

Cut the box away from the ice cream. Place the ice cream in the middle of a clean table. Add the toppings to it, making a huge sundae. After blindfolding everyone, give each person a spoon and feed the huge table sundae to your date. You'll probably want to wear towels as bibs.

Timed Lego Building

Borrow a box of Legos, and divide them evenly among the participating couples. Each couple has ten minutes to build a creation out of Legos. If there are a lot of you, you may need to use two boxes of Legos.

Treasure Hunt

For this group date, you will need someone to make a map and bury a treasure chest for you that is filled with items such as blankets, snacks, and board games. An ice chest or cooler makes a great treasure chest for this date. You can make your map look old and authentic by holding a flame an inch or two below the paper to brown it and singe the edges.

Each couple meets at your house for the date, where you have previously gathered pirate clothing such as headbands, eye patches, and swords for everyone to wear. Reveal to the rest of the pirates that you have found a secret map containing clues to help you locate a hidden treasure.

Caravan to a nearby beach or lake, taking with you your map and a few small shovels. Following the clues on your map, locate the spot of the hidden treasure and dig it out of the sand. Open the treasure chest and find the "treasures" inside that you will use to enjoy the rest of your evening together on the beach.

Variation: This treasure hunt can also be done during the winter. The treasure chest can be easily hidden in a snow bank.

Un-Birthday Party

Invite some couples over to celebrate everyone's un-birthday. Play party games and make an un-birthday cake for everyone to share. Ask each couple to bring a gift from the dollar store. Exchange gifts between couples. Remember, you can only come if it isn't your birthday.

Video Scavenger Hunt

For this group date, split up into teams and borrow a home-video camera for each team. Give each team a list of things to film on their camera. Some ideas for the list: a bird in flight, a waiter from a hotel restaurant, someone from your team standing on a diving board, or a car stopping at a stop sign.

Variation: To make this more challenging, require each team to film events rather than just objects. Give points for each event recorded, based on the difficulty of recording it. For example: man walking down street with dog (five points), woman throwing money into a fountain (ten points), car pulled over by policeman (fifteen points), policeman pulling you over (minus fifteen points).

Water Balloon Volleyball

Play a wet version of volleyball, where the volleyball is a water balloon and each couple uses a towel held between them to catch and toss the water balloon. Dress for wet.

Water Trough Softball

For this group date requiring about eight couples, borrow three rubber watering troughs from a farmer. Also, obtain the necessary equipment to play softball. The water troughs will serve as the bases. Cover the area from third base to home plate with a plastic tarp with water running on it so you can "slide" into home. Play the game just like normal softball, except that the runner has to jump into the filled water troughs instead of stepping on the bases as he approaches them.

Water Volleyball

To play this game on a group date, make a water volleyball court by lining an outside volleyball court with sand bags. Spread black plastic over both the volleyball court and the sand bags. Put more sand bags on top of the plastic-covered sandbags, sandwiching the plastic in between. Then, fill the court with water and play volleyball on this slippery surface. Make sure you use a synthetic volleyball, since it will get wet, and as in any water game, use caution on the slippery surface of the playing court.

Variation: Set up a volleyball net over a swimming pool and play water volleyball. For an additional challenge, cover the net with black plastic and play blind volleyball: you only see the ball when it comes above the net.

Water War

For this group date, borrow enough water guns so that each person has one to use. Go to a large playing field, divide into teams, set boundaries, and have a water war with your water guns.

Watermelon Bam-ball

To play this version of softball on a group date, collect each couple's dollar and purchase a watermelon. Cut it into thin slices and place several slices at each base on your softball diamond. Divide into teams and play softball, adding the rule that as each runner approaches a base, she must stop, eat a slice of watermelon, and deposit the rind into a bucket near the base before running to the next base.

Who's Who?

This date requires two or more couples. The objective of the date is to not only have fun, but to learn interesting things about each other. The format is very simple: each person writes down one true thing about himself that the others probably wouldn't know. Each person also writes down one false thing about himself on the paper as well. The papers are then given to one person who reads them one at a time to the group. The group attempts to guess who the person is from the two clues given. The group must also guess which fact is true and which one is false. When the group has attempted to guess who the person is, the actual person comes forward.

Variation: Using a similar method, learn about how each couple met. Have one person in the couple tell the truth about how the two met and the other give a fictional account. The group attempts to figure out which member of the couple is telling the truth and which is not.

Chapter Three

Single or Group Dates

Around The World

For this dizzying game, you need access to a ping pong table and people with fast hands. Around the world can be played with two or more people. To play, divide the group into two equal lines, each line standing behind a lead person at each end of the ping pong table. The two leaders have a paddle and one has the ball. The leader of team #1 serves the ball. Immediately after serving the ball, he drops the paddle onto the table and runs to the end of his line, while the person directly behind him takes the paddle and prepares to receive the ball from the leader of team #2. The leader of team #2 receives the ball from the leader of team #1 and returns the serve to the next player of team #1. He then drops his paddle, runs to the end of his line, and the person who was directly behind him takes his place.

If any team member hits the net, misses the ball, or fails to hit the ball onto the other team's side of the table during his turn at the table, he gets a strike. When any person on either team gets a total of three strikes, he is out of the game. Play continues until only two people are left.

Art Appraising

Take your date to either a museum, an art gallery, or an art exhibit. Examine the art together and try to appraise it on your own before looking at the price tag.

Backwards Date

Plan an inexpensive date and then do as much of the date as possible backwards. For example, if you are a girl, drive the car and pick up your date. When you pick him up, pull into the driveway in reverse and walk backwards to the door. If your date takes place in the evening, you could eat a cold cereal breakfast instead of dinner. You could even wear your clothes backwards. At the door, one of you could jokingly say, "Well, I don't usually kiss on the first date, but since it's a backwards date..."

Bottling Fruit

Previous to this date, suggest to your parents that if they contribute the necessary materials and teach you how to bottle fruit, you and your date will contribute the labor. You might bottle peaches, pears, apricots, pickles, or whatever is in season.

Note: Pears can often be obtained from orchards for free. While green and hard, many of them are knocked off the trees. Ask the owner of the orchard if you can collect the fallen pears. These pears will ripen within a few days.

Build a Tree House

Gather together scrap boards, nails, a saw, and a hammer. Then find a good, strong tree in which you have obtained permission to build a tree house. For the date, design and build your own tree house. When your house is complete, sit in it and eat snacks, play games, or read stories. Some appropriate stories may be *Tom Sawyer, Huckleberry Finn, The Swiss Family Robinson,* or *Tarzan*.

Catered Picnic In A Cave

For this date, locate a small shallow cave. Prior to the date, check the cave for structural soundness, making certain there are no dangers present such as pits, snakes, or animals. Invite your date to go hiking with you, but don't tell her that you'll be going to a cave.

Bribe a younger brother or sister to act as a waiter or waitress. Send your waiter to the cave to set up a candlelight dinner with a stereo for romantic music, blankets to sit on, and some snacks. When he's done, he should hide outside the cave, ready to bring in the snacks at your request. When you and your date arrive at the cave (which just happens to be on the trail that you're hiking), take your date in to explore the cave. Light the candles, listen to music, and when you're hungry, snap your fingers and little brother will come in all dressed up to serve your picnic.

Variation: If you can't find a cave, choose any scenic spot. Lay down a picnic blanket, turn on some soft music, and when you're hungry, just snap your fingers. Out of the bushes, your "waiter" comes with candles, silverware, and a simple meal.

Children's Books

Make books for children with your date. Begin by making up a children's story together and writing it on sheets of paper. Then illustrate the sheets by drawing pictures or cutting out pictures from magazines. Take the books to the children's center of a hospital and read them to the children.

Variation: Make puppets out of paper lunch sacks or other materials. Write a story together with your puppets as the characters. Then perform a puppet show for children.

Coloring Contest

Give each other an equal number of pages to color from a coloring book. After coloring them, have a child judge your work to see which ones he or she likes the best.

Compass Hike

Instead of just going on a hike, offer a little challenge by turning it into an orientation course, using a compass as your guide. If you don't know how to use a compass, spend the first hour or so of your date learning how to use it. Then have someone set up a compass course for you to follow on your hike.

Cookies-N-Kids

Since cookies and kids have always been a perfect combination, this date involves both. Make a batch of cookies with your date and take it to the children's floor of a hospital. After getting approval from the children's nurses, give the cookies to the young patients. While visiting, you could also read to the children.

Costume Competition

Challenge your date to dress in a funnier costume than you will wear for this date, but don't let her know what your costume will be. When you pick up your date, take her to a public place (such as a shopping mall) and ask strangers to vote on whose costume is funnier. You might want to video tape some of the responses.

Current Events Quiz

This date will test your knowledge of what's going on in the world. Gather a few national or world news magazines. Divide them evenly among the participants. Take twenty five to thirty minutes to read and compile a list of trivia questions about current events. Quiz each other using these questions. If the questions seem too difficult, swap magazines and allow ten minutes to review the magazines before trying to answer the questions. Keep score if you're feeling competitive.

Dance Lessons

Invite an older couple to teach you and your date how to dance to the music of their era. If they are willing, teach them how to dance to your music as well.

Department Store Movie

After obtaining permission from the store manager, take your date to a department store that sells televisions and ask the store clerk to play a video for you and your date or group. With the store's approval, you could also take along bean bags or something soft to sit on.

Deserted Island Dinner

Invite your date to a deserted island for dinner. Take

her to a wide, safe, grassy median in the middle of two streets. Set up a card table, set the table, light some candles, and eat an inexpensive dinner. If you really want to get fancy, arrange for a "waiter" to set everything up and serve you.

Entrepreneur Night

Here's a date for those of you who are business minded. See how much money you can legally and safely earn during the date. If it's a group date, compete with other couples to see which couple can earn the most money. Some ideas are cleaning rain gutters, raking leaves, chopping wood, or washing cars. When you have earned your money, you could use it to purchase refreshments or donate it to a worthwhile charity in your area.

Environmental Date

All you need is a date and a trash bag. Spend the evening picking up trash in a recreational area, along a highway median, or wherever you find the need.

Evening With The Elderly

Take a blank tape, a tape recorder, and a plate of homemade cookies to an elderly person's house or a convalescent center. Choose elderly people who would like to talk with you, and ask them to tell you about themselves. With their permission, record your conversations with them on your cassette recorder. After your visit, return to your house and write or type up a written record of the conversation. For another date, visit them again and present them with their own personal history which you have recorded.

Note: It may be helpful to have some specific questions prepared in advance to get the conversation started. For example, "Tell us about your favorite childhood memory."

Exploring the Old Frontier

Obtain several stories from pioneer journals or history books and read them together. Then, take your date to a once-inhabited pioneer dwelling such as an old cabin or even a "ghost town." If necessary, obtain permission from the landowners before exploring the old buildings. Look for pioneer artifacts and imagine what pioneer life would have been like. If permitted, you might try to locate old dumping grounds and search them for buttons, glass bottles, pieces of china, coins, or other objects, using a shovel to turn the soil. Be extremely cautious around all old buildings, as many of them are no longer stable.

Family Cabin Date

If you have a family cabin or have access to one, invite your date to join you and your family at the cabin. Play games with the family, go on nature hikes, fish, or do whatever else your family enjoys.

Farm Date

For this date, take your date to a farm and carry out farm chores together. For example, you might milk cows, bottle-feed lambs, saddle and ride horses, drive tractors, or feed the chickens.

Feed The Birds

Ducks frequent many ponds and other bodies of water in city parks and are always on the lookout for a handout. Some parks, however, prohibit feeding the ducks. Find one that allows it, buy an inexpensive loaf of bread, and feed the ducks together. If it's winter, make homemade bird feeders to feed smaller birds.

Directions for making a simple bird feeder: spread peanut butter on a pine cone and stick a small amount of bird seed to the peanut butter. Tie a piece of yarn from the top of the pine cone to a tree branch.

Fiddler On The Roof

For this date, invite your date to a movie. In advance, carefully carry a television, a video cassette recorder, and something comfortable to sit on, onto your roof. Then, with your date, climb up onto the roof and watch the movie, "Fiddler On The Roof." Before going on this date, make sure that the weather is clear and that your roof is strong enough to support everything.

Football Cookies and Football Games

If you and your date or group like football, get together before a football game to make football cookies. Make your favorite recipe, but cut the dough with a homemade football-shaped cookie cutter. To make the cutter, bend opposite sides of the rim of an opened tin outward until it makes the shape of a football. Be sure to bend any sharp edges inward with pliers and wash the can well before using it. When the cookies are done, settle in for the game and eat your cookies together.

Foreign Flight Night

For this date, decorate a room of your house to look like a foreign country and invite your date to go with you on a trip to a foreign country for the evening. When you are both in the car, insert a pre-recorded tape of the voice of a captain of an airplane welcoming the passengers aboard and wishing you an enjoyable flight to your destination. You could also record the sound of an airplane taking off. Then, drive away from your date's house and go back to your house. Upon arrival, play a recording of an airplane landing and some last words from the captain. At your house, welcome your date to the "foreign country." Listen to cultural music, play foreign games, and read about the country. If you want to include dinner, serve an inexpensive meal of foreign food.

Free Concert

You can spend thirty dollars or more taking your date to an outdoor concert in the summer or you can save all that money and still hear the performance and possibly see the band. How? Attend the concert on the outside of the stadium. Set up lawn chairs or blankets outside on the lawn or parking lot. The music will be almost as audible outside as inside.

Free Movie

Schedule a viewing room at a public library. Take your date to the library, check out a movie, and watch it together in your private little theater.

Frisbee Golf

Select a nice, grassy area with several trees around (or set up several straight posts in the grass). Tie a red ribbon around each tree to make it clearly visible, as each tree will represent one hole of golf. Give each player a frisbee.

To play this game, take turns throwing your frisbees

at each tree, marking one stroke for each throw. Each throw should move your frisbee closer to the tree, because you make the second throw from where the first throw landed. As in golf, the lowest score wins. The length of the game is determined by the number of trees you choose to mark.

Help The Homeless

Volunteer with your date to help serve the homeless at one of the homeless shelters in town. This date is especially meaningful on a special day.

Hobo Dinner

Prepare a meal together around a campfire. You could heat up chili, stew, or meat and potatoes wrapped in aluminum foil. For a group date, have each couple bring a different ingredient to use in making a stew.

Homemade Ice Cream

This works best as a group date but can be done with just two people. Assign each couple to bring an ingredient in a recipe to make homemade ice cream. For the date, make the ice cream together at someone's home or at a park.

Ice Blocking

Purchase a block of ice from a supermarket. Take your date to the top of a grassy hill, put a towel on the ice, sit together on it, and slide down the hill. For a group date, have each couple purchase a block of ice and race down the hill. Check with local authorities to be certain there are no ordinances against this type of activity before planning the date.

Joke Book

If you're the kind of person that finds yourself laughing harder at your own jokes than anyone else, this date is for you. Get a paper and pen and co-author an original joke book together. After all, few things are as satisfying as a belly ache caused by laughing at your own jokes.

Leftover Delight

This date is ideal for the penny-pinching college student. Invite your date over for dinner but tell him that he must bring all of his leftovers from his refrigerator with him. For the date, use all of yours and your date's leftovers to create the best leftover delight ever. Since this date will cost you no money, you could rent a dollar video for after dinner or make an inexpensive dessert.

Liquid Only Date

The object of this date is to do as many things using liquids as possible. For a meal, make sure you eat liquids such as soup or cold cereal. If you're brave, throw some food into the blender and liquify it. For an activity, play liquid games. For example, you could go swimming, have a water-balloon toss, or fill a baby bottle with water and race to see who can suck it dry the fastest.

Magic Show

Magic fascinates adults as well as children. It can be surprisingly simple to learn a few amazing tricks. Check out a magic book from the library. With your date or group, learn some tricks and practice them on each other. When you're ready to perform, take your act to a rest home, a children's hospital, a day care center, or a homeless shelter and astound an audience with your newly acquired abilities.

Make and Fly Kites

On a windy day, use light wood and black plastic from garbage bags to make a kite. When you're finished, fly it together.

Mall Picnic

Ask your date to go to lunch with you at the mall. Bring a picnic lunch and portable stereo. When you get there play soft music and have a picnic in the food court.

Marriage Preparation Date

Invite your date to dinner. But first, take her to a supermarket and decide on ingredients which cost no more than a dollar, with which you will make the most delicious dinner possible. If you are with a group, have each couple purchase a dollar's worth of food for a different part of the meal. Then, go back to your house, prepare the meal together, and enjoy!

Marshmallow Fireside

Ask your date to go to a "fireside" with you. This fireside, however, will be held outdoors so dress casually and warmly. After you pick up your date, drive to the mountains, build a fire, and listen to a youth speaker on cassette tape as you roast marshmallows.

Mechanic Night

This date is not only educational but can be money-saving as well. The purpose of the date is to learn about cars together or to share your mechanical knowledge with your date. If you are beginners, you could learn how to change a tire, check the oil, and fill the windshield wiper fluid container. If you are more advanced in the field of auto maintenance, learn how to change the oil or replace a belt. Be sure your date knows the nature of this activity beforehand, so he or she can dress appropriately.

Mini-Dinner Date

For this date, prepare a meal in which everything is miniature. For example, eat with miniature spoons from a yogurt store or with toothpicks instead of chopsticks. You could eat mini-sausages, peas, mini-ice cream cones, mini-cookies, or roasted mini-marshmallows over a birthday candle.

Modern Fairy Tales

With your date, select a favorite fairy tale. Then, look through old magazines to find pictures that depict scenes from your fairy tale. Glue these pictures onto sturdy pieces of paper and create a homemade story book. To complete the project, write the words of the story underneath your pictures. When you are finished, read the stories to younger brothers and sisters or gather the neighborhood children together and read to them.

Movie In The Woods

Check out a 16-millimeter film and a movie projector from your local library and borrow a generator from someone you know. Outside in the trees, choose a comfortable area for bean bags or blankets for chairs and set up the movie projector. Hang a white sheet from the trees as a movie screen and watch your movie together. Use a VCR if a movie projector is not available.

Munchy Lunchy

O.K., so there's really no such thing as a free lunch; however, this date is about as close as you can get to one. Under the guise of shopping, become professional taste testers. Wander from aisle to aisle in a grocery store, sampling the various foods offered. Comment on flavor, richness, texture, and ingredients. You'll be munchy connoisseurs before you know it.

Mystery Camp-out

Before this date, set up a tent in your back yard. Fix an inexpensive dinner and put it inside the tent along with some board games. When you pick up your date, blindfold her and drive her around town, asking her to guess where you are taking her. After arriving at your house, guide her into the back yard, and to the tent before you take off the blindfold. Eat dinner together and play games inside the tent. When you are finished, have your date guess where you are. Take her outside the tent and watch her surprise as she realizes you are in your back yard!

Name That Tune

Isn't it amazing how quickly musical groups come and go? Music doesn't need to be very old to be out of style. Test your knowledge of the trends in music by playing a version of the classic "Name That Tune." Each person brings old music C.D.'s, cassette tapes, eight tracks, or records. Play a tune and time how long it takes the others to recognize it. If this is a group date, see who can "Name That Tune" first. Give one of your old music albums to the winner.

Newspaper Logging

Make newspaper logs together. Soak newspapers in a tub of water with about one cup of laundry detergent. Roll the newspapers onto a broomstick until they make a log about four inches thick. Remove the broomstick and stand the logs on end to dry. After they dry (days later), try them out in a fire or give them to people in your area who need fuel for wood burning stoves.

Old-Fashioned Fishing

Two hooks, two lines, and a pocket knife are all you need for this "Huckleberry Finn" type date. Go to a favorite fishing spot and try your luck at fishing the old-fashioned way: make your own fishing poles out of tender saplings, tie your line, and hook on whatever type of bait you can find.

Old Swimmin' Hole

Invite your date to go swimming. Take her to your favorite swimming hole in a stream or river. Swim (don't dive), catch crayfish, find freshwater mussels, float the river on inner tubes, or have a water fight.

Reverse Tie-Dyeing

Dyeing shirts is not only fun but gives you and your date a matching outfit for future dates. Reverse tie dyeing takes colors out of a shirt instead of putting new colors onto one. Select an old colored T-shirt from each of your wardrobes. Twist each T-shirt as tightly as you can, and bind it with rubber bands or tightly tied string. Wearing rubber gloves, immerse the shirts in a bucket of hot water containing two cups of household liquid bleach. Watch the colors being released from the shirts. Stir the shirts occasionally, adding more bleach if desired. When the desired fade is achieved, place the shirts in a washing machine and run them through a normal wash and rinse cycle. When the rinse cycle is finished, remove the rubber bands or string from your shirts and let them dry.

Sand Castles and Sea Shells

Take pails, scoops, and your date or group to a sandy beach to build a sand castle. If the beach is next to an ocean, collect sea shells to make sea shell decorations such as necklaces, painted sand dollars, and shell people.

Variation: If there isn't a beach nearby, collect smooth rocks. Then glue them together and paint them to make rock people.

Sesame Street Surprise

Invite your date over to watch an "exciting, action-packed, non-violent, educational, G-rated movie." Pop some popcorn and put in a video of two hours of previously-recorded *Sesame Street* programs. Compete with each other to see who can name the most Sesame Street characters.

Silent Night

This date will test your ability to communicate with your date without using words. Because verbal communication is extremely important in dating, this one should probably not be used on a first date! The object of this date is for both of you to be completely silent for as much of the evening as possible. You could check out silent movies from a library and show them for part of the activity. You might play board games without ever verbally communicating during the game. If you're on a group date, try competing against the other couples to see who can talk the least. If it seems too difficult to never talk, allow for one-minute talk periods every thirty minutes.

Skip-A-Rock

Find several good skipping rocks and take your date or group to an area where there is a large body of smooth water. Hold a rock skipping contest. After skipping rocks, swim, wade, fish, or float on tubes in the water.

Variation: For a group date, have a contest to see who can skip rocks the farthest with beginner and advanced categories.

Sledding

Find a nice, steep slope with lots of snow and take your date or group sledding. Bring a thermos of hot chocolate to warm yourselves afterwards.

Snow Golf

Find an open, snow-covered space suitable for snow golf. Make holes in the snow for golf holes and set up poles with numbered flags on them. Then, play snow golf using brightly colored golf balls.

Snowshoeing

Part of the fun of going snowshoeing is making your own snowshoes first. Lids to five gallon plastic buckets make wonderful snowshoes. After obtaining two lids per person, you must figure out how to attach them to your feet. Remember: your feet will be inside of boots while snowshoeing.

There are several ways to attach your foot to the lid; only one method is mentioned here. Place your boot on a lid and make a slit just off to the side of the boot on each side. It should be big enough to slide a strap through. Pull the strap over your boot and tie it on.

When everything is ready, try your luck at stomping around in the snow. Pack a light lunch, make a table and chairs out of snow, and enjoy a picnic in a winter wonderland.

Snow Shoveling

After a fresh snowfall, ask your date or group over to help you shovel the driveways of some families in your neighborhood. Come in for hot chocolate afterwards and play games.

Sock Puppets

Every home seems to have a secret little monster that lives in the clothes dryer that eventually eats one sock from every pair. With the remaining matchless socks, create sock puppets. Sew eyes, nose, hair, mouth, and ears on with a needle and thread. Give them names and create a story in which they are the characters. Then perform a puppet show for children.

Special Olympics Date

In many areas, volunteers are needed to help handicapped people perform different activities in the Special Olympics program. Call you local Special Olympics chapter (or any other program for the handicapped in your area) and volunteer yourself and your date or group to assist with one of their activities.

Squirt Art

It seems that only a handful of people have ever experienced the joys of winter squirt art. Hopefully you will become one of them. Fill squirt bottles and squirt guns with water. Add a different color of food coloring to each bottle. You are now ready to create art, using the snow as your canvas. After dressing warmly, go outside and squirt your colored water into the snow, making whatever designs you desire.

Star Search

Take your date or group to a public library and become familiar with different star constellations. Try to determine which constellations are currently visible in your area. Then, find a place where you can get a clear view of the stars and search for the constellations together.

Straw Creations

Using a box of plastic drinking straws, build straw creations together. If you decide to use glue in your structures, the object of the date is to work together to create a structure of your choice, using only one box of plastic drinking straws and some glue. If, however, you decide not to use glue, then turn the date into a contest. Have each person create a separate structure, trying to use as many drinking straws as possible in his or her structure.

Tin Foil Dinner

Fill sheets of tinfoil (shiny side in) with vegetables such as carrots, potatoes, and onions. Add a raw hamburger patty seasoned with whatever you like, and wrap the tinfoil around the mixture completely. A second layer of tinfoil wrapped around the mixture (shiny side in also) will help prevent burning. Put the dinners in the red hot coals of a campfire and listen to them sizzle. Turn them every few minutes, checking them frequently until the ingredients inside are completely cooked. When they're done, enjoy!

Toilet Paper Date

Get a roll of toilet paper and some pens to write stories, jokes, notes, and other messages on. Either send them to a long-distance friend by mail or deliver them to someone in the hospital to cheer him or her up.

Underwater Golf

Play miniature golf in either a swimming pool, a wading pool, or any other clear, shallow body of water (swimming pools with cement floors work best). Use golf clubs, golf balls, and weighted cups lying on their sides as the holes. If it is a nice, hot day and you don't mind getting completely wet, make your game more challenging by having one of the cups in the deep end.

Urban Camp-out

Set up a small tent inside your house. After your date or group arrives, roast hot dogs and marshmallows over either an outdoor grill or in your fireplace. Then for a hike, take your date on a walk through the neighborhood. When you return to your tent, sing campfire songs and play board games.

Wash Your Cars

For this date, wash your cars in your driveway instead of at a car wash. Vacuum them also. Be prepared for the almost inevitable water fight.

White Date

For this date, plan a fun and inexpensive evening with your date while focusing on the color white. For example, you should both dress in total white and drive a white car if you have one. Eat only white food such as white tortillas with white cheese, a side order of white beans, and milk to drink. Eat on white plates. Planning the date is just as fun as the date itself, and of course, if you don't like white, just follow these same rules using a different color.

Winter Drive-in Movie

Invite your date to a "drive-in movie" in the middle of winter, when drive-in movie theaters are closed. Check out a film projector and films from a public library. Pick up your date, drive into your garage, put the film projector on top of your car, and show the movie on the garage wall. You might get your parents to have hot chocolate and snacks prepared from inside the house as well.

Winter Picnic

Tell your date in advance to dress warmly for this date. Take him on a picnic in the snow. Stomp out a small picnic area, build a small cooking fire, and roast hot dogs and marshmallows together. You might also want to heat water for hot chocolate.

Would You Like A Penny?

That's an uncommon, ridiculous question, isn't it? It's amazing to see the many different reactions such a question can produce. Try it yourself. Cash in a dollar for a hundred pennies and give them away for this date. You might videotape the proceedings from a distance and watch it at home later. Keep a tally of how many people accept and how many reject the money.

Chapter Four

Single Dates

Aerobics

Nothing strengthens a romance like being in perfect step with each other throughout an entire aerobic workout video (I'm kidding of course). It does mark a significant achievement in your relationship, however, when you can sweat (or glisten, if you're a lady), take your pulse, and flex your muscles in front of your date. Check out an exercise video from the library or borrow one from a friend, dress in aerobic gear, and work out together.

Amateur Artists

Everyone has some degree of artistic ability; here's an opportunity to show yours. Dig out the old crusty watercolor set you used in third grade, and moisten it up again with a drop or two of water. Take your date, your watercolors, some thick paper, two paint brushes, and a rinse cup to a scenic area nearby and paint pictures of the landscape which surrounds you. If there are spectators watching you, talk with foreign accents, pretending to be famous artists. When you're finished, autograph one and present it to a spectator for free.

Berries and Syrup

Different types of berries grow in different locations, but chances are that if you live near the country there are delicious, edible berries growing in the wild. Find out what berries grow in your area and when they are in season. Pick some berries with your date and then make fresh syrup out of them. Since pancakes are good for either breakfast, lunch, or dinner, you could make pancakes afterwards, using your very own syrup. Possible edible berries in your area which make berry yummy syrup are currant berries, service berries, chokecherries, raspberries, blackberries, and blueberries.

Bicycling Tour

Ride bikes together through the countryside or the city where you live. Have races and make obstacle courses. If you get tired, have a turtle race instead: pace off a certain distance and time each other to see who can take the most time getting to the finish line without touching either his feet to the ground or going outside the narrow boundaries.

Bird Watching

Take your date and a pair of binoculars to a place where there are many species of birds. Wildlife refuges or waterways attract different varieties of waterfowl and birds of prey. Watch the birds and try to identify them according to their markings and mannerisms. You may want to take along an information book about birds.

Birthday History

If someone were to ask you what important events occurred in the world or in your community on the day you were born, what would you tell them? Wouldn't you feel terribly ashamed if you couldn't tell them anything? I wouldn't either, but here's a fun date just in case that question is asked of you during your lifetime.

Go to the periodicals section of a public library. Search for and find the newspapers that were printed on each of your birthdays, then read about the important events which occurred on the days you were born.

Card House Constructing

Obtain a deck of playing cards. With your date, see what kinds of structures you can make by stacking cards on their edges. You can make mazes, houses, and cars, for example. If you keep accidentally bumping the table or blowing the cards down, retire from card-building and play the card game instead.

Catching Butterflies

Make a butterfly net with your date by curling a wire hanger into a circle and twisting the ends back together to make a handle. Then, tape the opening of a transparent bread bag to the wire circle for a net. Use your net to catch butterflies together. Try to identify the butterflies by their markings. Be careful not to rub the "dust" from the butterflies' wings while examining them through the bag.

Celebrity Spotting

It's amazing how many "celebrities" can be found right where you live. Take your date to a place where there are a lot of people, such as an airport, shopping mall, college campus, or busy city street. Watch the people strolling by. When you see a person that looks like a celebrity, say, "There goes (celebrity's name)," but don't tell your date which person you are referring to. Your date must then examine the people and attempt to pick out the celebrity look-a-like.

Cheerios At Sunrise

Pick up your date before sunrise and drive him or her to the top of a mountain to watch the sun rise. While you are there, eat a simple breakfast, such as Cheerios.

Variation: Ride bicycles early in the morning to a scenic area like the edge of a lake, a stream, or a park, then eat breakfast together.

Childhood Revisited

Revert to your childhood and play some of your favorite games together. These games might include "Cowboys and Indians," "Cops and Robbers," computer games, dolls, jump rope, marbles, jacks, or hopscotch.

Cloud Breaking

On a cloudy day, take your date outside, spread out a blanket, and sit down. As you sit there, use your imagination to visualize objects in the clouds. Try to predict where the clouds will break and when they do, try to form new objects.

Compose Music

If you and your date are both musically inclined, bring your voices, your favorite instruments, and your creative abilities together and compose a song, with or without lyrics. Record your masterpiece on a cassette tape for future listening.

Computer Games

If you have access to both a home computer and some computer games on diskettes, find out what kinds of games your date likes to play and then challenge her to a competitive game or work with her on a cooperative game.

Coupon Date

A couple of weeks before this date, hand-craft a coupon with which you will ask someone on a date. It may say something like, "This coupon is good for one unforgettable date with (your name). It is redeemable on any one of the following dates (list a few nights you are free). To redeem this coupon call (your name) at (your phone number). Upon redeeming this coupon, you will receive three dates to choose from at the manufacturer's expense."

After your date calls to redeem the coupon, give him three other coupons, each for a different activity; for example, miniature golf. Let him redeem whichever coupon he would like. If all goes well, then you might allow him to keep the other two coupons and redeem them at a later date.

Driftwood Carving

Take your date on a nature walk along a lake shore or river bank, collecting pieces of driftwood as you go. Then, using pocket knives, sandpaper, or other tools, carve the driftwood into things such as earrings, staffs, canes, or spoons.

Fifty Wishes

For this date, give yourself and your date a roll of

fifty pennies. Go to a wishing well or a public fountain in which monetary donations are contributed and take turns making a wish and throwing a penny into the water. Make wishes until your pennies are gone.

Genealogy

Take your date to the nearest public library (or family history center if there is one in town) and research information about your and your date's ancestors. It would be helpful to take family information such as pedigree charts, family group records, or journals with you to help you get started. With a librarian's help, use census records, certificates of birth, marriage and death, and other important resources to collect information. Make sure to document the information you find for your family's future reference.

Grocery Shopping

For this date, you don't have to spend a dime of your own money—spend someone else's for a change. Go grocery shopping together for mom and dad or for an elderly neighbor.

House Shopping

Before you get married, it's fun to pretend that you're married and go house-shopping together. Look through a newspaper to find the open houses in your area. Decide which ones you want to attend and go house-hunting. Have fun with it. Flush the toilets, test the faucets, talk interest rates, etc. If it's a very expensive house, play the part by mentioning where you would park which Mercedes and where the maid's quarters would be, or ask how close the nearest yacht storage is.

Impress the Parents Date

For this activity, invite your date to collaborate with you in a service project for her parents. If she agrees, call her parents and ask them if you and their daughter could give them an evening to themselves, free of their other children. Then for the date, take their children to a park and then to your house for a video, food, and games.

Variation: Mothers of newborn babies frequently need help with little things around the house. Volunteer some time for you and your date to help wash the dishes, prepare a meal, or take her other children out for a few hours to let her relax.

Journal Reading

Warning! The contents of this date could prove to be extremely embarrassing. This date is not recommended for couples who do not share a great deal of commitment. Proceed at your own risk.

Read your journals to each other. Share what you wrote about your first date with each other and subsequent dates that you have been on with them. Randomly pick a date from the past and read what each of you did that day. Using your journals, tell each other what you received for Christmas when you were seven, who your favorite music groups were, what foods you hated, and so on. Read your own journal so that you can scan the pages before reading them aloud, unless it contains no embarrassing material!

Mad Poetry

Depending on your relationship and the mood you're in, this evening together can be either romantic or ridiculous. Write poetry together, taking turns writing every other line. Start with a title and then let your date write the first line of the poem. If you don't have a knack for poetry, you could write a story in the same fashion.

Nature Walk

From a public library, check out a book that identifies several forms of wildlife and fauna in your area. Take your date to either a park, a river, a lake, a wetland, a desert, or a mountain where you can find and identify some of the plants and animals in the book.

Night-Crawler Hunting

In many areas in spring, summer, and fall, night crawlers (large earthworms) come out at night and sprawl across the lawn or dirt. Catching them can be a slimy thrill, especially if you're going fishing the next day. All you need is a flashlight, a bucket with a few inches of dirt and leaves in it, sharp eyes, and fast fingers. Scan the ground slowly with the flashlight. When you see a shiny, slimy night-crawler, grab the end of it that is nearest to it's hole and then slowly ease it out of the ground.

Patchwork Project

This date will help you or someone you know prepare to make a patchwork quilt by acquiring enough squares of material to make a quilt top. To obtain the necessary materials, go on a patch hunt, asking neighbors for old material scraps or old articles of clothing or sheets that they no longer need. When you have collected enough material, cut the pieces of fabric into squares. Then, if you have time, sew the squares together to form a quilt top.

Pet Store

Many people love to watch animals, especially puppies and kittens at play. For this date, go to a pet store and watch the animals. If the store manager allows it, you may even hold some of them. You might want to call several pet stores beforehand to find out which ones will allow you to touch the animals. Be sure to obey all store rules.

Variation: Visit the animals at the local animal shelter.

Pickup Picnic

Put a small table and two folding chairs in the back of a pickup truck and prepare an inexpensive picnic. Ask your date to go to lunch with you. Take them to the mountains or to any other outside location. Set up the table and chairs in the back of the truck and eat your picnic lunch.

Variation: During the winter, take the rear seats out of a van and have your picnic inside the van instead of in the back of a truck.

Picture Show

Invite your special someone over for an old-fashioned picture show. To participate, he must bring some pictures in an old photo album. Swap albums and write captions for the pictures on slips of paper. Take turns sharing the captions you've created. Compare what each of you was doing at a certain age in life. Match up your school pictures with your date's from when you were the same age to see what a good match you have always made. (Did you both look great in braces?)

Plant a Garden

Plant a garden for either yourselves, your parents, or an elderly person. Prepare the land first by rotor-tilling it and fertilizing it if possible.

Price Is Right

This game can be played at any store, but is probably easiest to play at a grocery store. With a pad and paper, walk the aisles of the store. From a distance, pick out a product. Each of you guess the price of the item. Check the price. Scoring can be done in two ways. First, whoever guessed closest to the actual price scores a point. Second, you each calculate the difference between the true price and your guess and add that amount to your score. Lowest score wins.

Quilt Tying

If a family member or friend is making a quilt, get a date and help tie it. If you're preparing to propose to your date, this might help you tie the knot (HA! HA!).

Rainy Day Fun Day

It's not easy to plan for this date, since weather predictions aren't always reliable. I guess you could call the person and say, "Would you like to go out with me the next time it rains?" However, the best way is to keep this date in reserve in case a rainstorm begins to drown out your other plans.

When the rain begins to pour, make boats out of paper or a piece of wood. Race your boats down the street gutter. The fastest boat three out of five times wins. Go puddle jumping, seeing how many jumps it takes to empty a puddle. Lay on your backs on the grass, watching the raindrops plummet toward you and splash on your face. Put a plastic tarp out on the lawn for a slip and slide, or go down a slippery slide at the park. If you see lightning, go back inside and dry off and drink hot chocolate together.

Ramen Noodle Cuisine

Invite your date over for a contest to see which of you can prepare the most exquisite meal using ramen noodles as an ingredient. Remember not to spend over a dollar if you purchase additional ingredients.

Reception Crashing

Invite yourself and your date to a wedding reception in your area. Dress up for the occasion. Meet the bride and groom, pretending to be one of their childhood friends (it's really funny when they think they remember you). Eat cake and any other refreshments and dance to the music. When you're ready to leave, put your dollar on their money tree.

Rock Hunting

Take your date hunting for rocks. You could look for interesting looking rocks if you're an amateur, or you could look for specific minerals, fossils or other kinds of rocks if you're a more experienced rock hunter.

Roller Blading

Borrow a set of roller blades for yourself and a set for your date and roller blade together around a park. Be sure to wear protective padding and be careful.

Romantic Reading

On a cool winter night, build a fire in a fireplace, make some hot chocolate, and roast marshmallows. Afterward, snuggle up with a good book and read together. Depending on your mood, you could read comic books, short stories, or the scriptures, for example.

Sew Crazy

Ask someone who knows how to sew to give you and your date a five-minute lesson on the art of sewing. Then, using old sheets, blankets, or other scrap material, take turns sewing outfits for each other. If you don't have a sewing machine, simply use a needle and thread.

Tent City

For some strange reason, sitting underneath a blanket fascinates most humans. Share that fascination with your favorite non-claustrophobic person. Turn a room into a tent city together by draping blankets over various objects. Play board games, eat snacks, and enjoy each other's company under your blanket canopy. (Breath freshener is highly recommended).

This Is Your Life

Invite your date over for an evening with the family. What your date won't know, however, is that you have invited his family over as well. Previous to the date, ask your date's family to put together a lengthy presentation all about him. Have them include stories of his most embarrassing moments, his accomplishments, some awards he has received, and pictures of him. For the date, turn the time over to his family and let them share their presentation of your date's life story.

Toy Store Date

Go to a toy store and play with the display toys. Remember to be courteous to customers who would like to try out the display toys as well.

Trampoline and Whipped Cream

Buy two cans of the most inexpensive whipping cream you can find. Give your date a can of whipping cream and keep one for yourself. As you jump on the trampoline, have a whipping cream war. If it's hot, you could put a sprinkler head under the trampoline and soak yourselves and the trampoline.

Visit to a Friendly Stranger's House

This date will test your acting ability and your date's social skills like no other. Before the date, select one of your friends with a beautiful home and arrange with them to help you to create the following scenario. After you pick up your date, drive toward the theater. Ask her on the way, however, if she would like to do something "spontaneous" instead. Tell her that nearby is a beautiful home of which you have always wanted to see the inside. Persuade your date to join you in your quest to see it.

Park in front of the house and walk up to the doorway. Peer in the windows to see if anyone is home and see how your date reacts. Ring the doorbell. When the door opens, look at your date, urging her to explain why you are there. If she fumbles, explain that you have always wanted to see the inside of this very beautiful house. After being invited in by the friendly "stranger," ask for a tour. The stranger happily consents, and proceeds to give you a full-blown tour of the home. They include details of its history, furniture, and decor. After the tour of the home, and to the continued embarrassment of your date, ask for a tour of the yard or garden. Again, the friendly stranger grants your request.

When the tour is completed, thank the stranger for their hospitality and head for the door. Just before leaving, however, ask for a drink of water. At this, the stranger invites you and your date into the kitchen for cookies and milk. Thank them again and mention that you were planning to take your date to see a movie, but that you decided to visit their home instead. The stranger expresses his sympathy that you missed your movie, and offers to let you watch a video in their home. During the movie, your host offers popcorn and drinks.

Sometime during the evening, your date will figure out that this friendly stranger is only a stranger to her, and that you set all of this up in advance. It should cause some laughs for days afterwards.

Who Dunnit?

Prior to this date, contact the federal court building in your area to find out when public trials are being held. Take your date to a live trial that looks interesting to watch. Watch the trial, weighing the evidence and arguments of both sides. Try to guess which way the jury or judge will decide.

Wilderness Scrabble

Take a Scrabble game with you and your date into the mountains. Play "Wilderness Scrabble" together, in which each word used must in some way relate to the surroundings that you are playing in. If it seems too difficult to create only words that have to do with nature, try using ten tiles each instead of seven during the game.

Wildflower Bouquets

Every Spring, wildflowers cast rainbows of color across the countryside. Share an afternoon enjoying the beauty of Spring with the person of your choice. Sniff wildflowers and see which of you gets hayfever the fastest (ha ha). Pick a multi-petaled flower (but don't pick your state flower) and pluck each petal off, telling each other one reason why you love him with each pluck of a petal. When you're ready to go home, pick a bouquet of wildflowers to take with you.

Yard Sale Date

Look in a local newspaper to find some yard sales that are scheduled for the day of your date. Give fifty cents to your date and keep fifty cents for yourself. Go with your date from yard sale to yard sale, looking at all the items for sale. Secretly purchase an item that you think will please your date the most and have her do the same. Then, after you've each bought a gift go back to your house to exchange them.

For additional fun shopping at yard sales, take a video camera with you and ask the people how much they're selling their yard or garage for. Videotape their responses and watch the tape later.

Variation: With your parent's permission, clean out your garage at home with your date and hold your own yard sale.

Chapter Five

Holiday Dates

Christmas Caroling

Get a group together and sing Christmas carols to friends, neighbors, or people in rest homes. You might make cookies to take to the people you visit. When you're all sung out, go back to someone's house for cookies and hot chocolate.

Christmas Tree Cutting

In some areas, when the Bureau of Land Management clears land, they will allow you to cut down one Christmas tree for free for every five non-Christmas trees you cut down for them. This makes for an ideal group date. You can cut down a tree either for a needy family or for your own family.

Christmas Tree Decorating

For this date, make your own Christmas tree ornaments. Collect supplies in advance such as wood chips, canning jar lids, candles, pine cones, popcorn, clay, and paper. You could put old pictures on the decorations to personalize them.

Variation: For a group date, assign each couple a

theme for its tree, such as "The Edible Tree" or "White Christmas."

Christmas Wreath Making

Beautiful, natural, fragrant Christmas wreaths can be made from a variety of evergreen boughs. Cut suitable boughs from available trees. Bend a wire hanger or other wire into a circle to form the wreath frame. Bend the boughs around the wire, connecting them to it with small pieces of craft wire. Add boughs according to taste. Decorate it with pine cones, red ribbon, bells, or other trinkets.

Easter Egg Hunt

Let's face it. Just because we got older doesn't mean we no longer enjoy the thrill of finding hidden Easter eggs. Treat yourselves to that thrill again. Shortly before Easter, buy a dozen or more eggs, boil them, and decorate them with your date. In addition to the traditional water-color Easter egg dyes, you could use craft paints to add detail to your eggs. If you're feeling competitive, give awards for the best-designed eggs. When the eggs are dry, let someone hide them for you, either in the house or outside in the yard. Then, see which couple can find the most eggs. Eat a few if you're hungry.

Easter Eggheads

Everyone's head is somewhat egg-shaped. That is to your advantage for this "egg-citing" date. Write the names of each person participating on slips of paper, place all the papers in a bowl, and have each participant draw one out. No one should reveal whose name he has drawn. The goal for the evening is for everyone to decorate a boiled egg to look like the person whose name he has drawn out of the bowl. Use paints, paper, crayons, or whatever else is available. When everyone is finished, try to match the people to the eggs.

Fourth of July Fireworks

For the next Fourth of July, look down on the fireworks instead of looking up at them. Take your date to the top of either a hill or a tall building. Spread out a blanket, drink soda, and enjoy the show.

Halloween Blind Date

On this date, neither you nor your date will know what the other looks like until the date is over. Have someone set you up with a person you don't know. Before the date, prepare a paper bag with eye holes and a mouth hole to wear on the date, and have your date do the same. When you pick her up, both of you should be wearing your paper bags on your heads. Then, you could go trick or treating, eat dinner, go to the park, or watch a movie, as long as you both wear your paper bags on your heads for the duration of the date. When you take your date home, reveal your faces to each other.

Halloween Spook Alley

Create a spook alley for the children in your neighborhood to attend. For a group date, have each couple bring a few ingredients to contribute to the spook alley. Some examples of ingredients are: peeled grapes in a bowl of liquid = eyeballs; spaghetti wrapped in cellophane = brains; a person underneath a box with his hand or head poking out of a hole in the box (this person looks dead at first, but wiggles as you go by). Set up the spook alley in your house, invite over the neighborhood children, and have fun!

Halloween Spooking

For this Halloween date, make your house as spooky as possible to try to scare the trick-or-treaters. Some ideas for making your house scary: stuff some old clothes with straw or rags to make a dummy and sit it on your front porch. Attach fishing line to it, and yank it to make it move as the trick-or-treaters approach. Or, play scary music through a window and hide in the bushes making scary noises. Be choosy who you try to scare. Small children are not good targets, but the older ones can often handle it.

Halloween Treating

Instead of going trick-or-treating on Halloween, just go treating. Dress up in your costumes and take homemade candies or cookies to your friends and neighbors.

Happy Holidays

This works best as a group date. Assign each couple a holiday to research with the purpose of discovering how its assigned holiday traditions really started. Then, as a group, sit around a fire or another comfortable setting, select a holiday, and have each couple relate a fictional version of how the traditions for that holiday started. After every couple has given its version, the couple who researched the holiday reveals the true origin of its traditions. Take turns revealing holiday stories until all the couples have shared what they have learned.

Natural Easter Egg Dyeing

How did people dye eggs for Easter before conventional dyes were invented? Naturally! You can do the same. Different colors of dye are found throughout nature, such as in plants and berries. The natural colors from these sources can often be extracted by boiling the plants or berries. The more concentrated the water, the darker the dye will be. Add or boil off water according to your preference. When the water is the color you desire, strain out the particles and let it cool. Dip in your boiled eggs to dye them. Some possible sources for dyes: strawberries or raspberries for red; blackberries or blueberries for blue; alfalfa or grass for green; dandelion heads or daffodil petals for yellow; marigold blossoms for orange.

Pumpkin Painting

For this date, buy some pumpkins and paint them into jack-o-lanterns using craft paints. When you are finished, take the pumpkins to a rest home and give them away.

Variation: Give each couple ten to twenty objects with which to decorate its pumpkin. Have someone judge the finished pumpkins.

Saint Patrick's Day Date

Have an all green date. Dress in all green and eat a green meal. Some ideas for the meal are green Jello salad, green fettucini, green peas, guacamole, green pancakes.

Santa's Elves

This date provides an opportunity for you and your date to participate in the spirit of giving this Christmas. A few weeks before Christmas, obtain some free scraps of wooden boards, preferably redwood, from a carpenter. You will use these to make a set of redwood building blocks for a child for Christmas. Find someone willing to let you and your date use his table saw. If you aren't familiar with how one works, have him help you. Carefully cut the wood scraps into squares, rectangles, and triangles of different sizes. If the edges of the blocks are too rough for a child, sand them lightly.

On Christmas Eve, wrap the set of blocks in wrapping paper and take it to the home of the child. Write the child's name on the package. Leave the gift on the doorstep, ring the doorbell, and run for cover!

Trick-or-Treating

This date is especially fun when it is done with a group. In the middle of summer, dig your Halloween costumes out of the closet and dress up as if it were actually Halloween. Go trick-or-treating to houses of your friends, requiring them to do a trick if they can't give you a treat.

Variation: On Halloween night, dress up in costumes and take your little brothers and sisters trick-or-treating.

Valentines to Eat

Here's a challenge and a change. Instead of giving valentine cards to each other this year, get together with your date and make edible valentines for each other instead. For example, make giant sugar cookies (as big as the cookie sheet), and write messages on them to each other with squeeze frosting (squeeze bags can be made by cutting a small hole in the corner of a zip-lock bag). Or, make edible valentines and give them away to family members and friends for Valentine's Day.